Becoming A Spirit-Empowered Evangelist

Library of Congress Control Number: 2016955580

ISBN: 978-1-63308-246-5 (hardback)
       978-1-63308-247-2 (paperback)
       978-1-63308-248-9 (ebook)

Interior and Cover Design by R'tor John D. Maghuyop

CHALFANT ECKERT
PUBLISHING

1028 S Bishop Avenue, Dept. 178
Rolla, MO 65401

Printed in United States of America

Dr. Marshall M. Windsor, DMin

Becoming A Spirit-Empowered Evangelist

CHALFANT ECKERT
PUBLISHING

TABLE OF CONTENTS

APPRECIATION

This book would have no reason for existence if it were not for all the men and women who have answered the call to evangelistic ministry—and who I currently represent as the General Presbyter for Assemblies of God evangelists. The daily sacrifices and suffering that many have willingly endured for the sake of the Gospel cannot be expressed in words alone. Their reward will far exceed any earthly attempt to provide something comparable.

I would also like to thank the many leaders within the Assemblies of God fellowship. The fellowship, opportunities to serve, and timely words of encouragement during valley experiences kept me in the ministry when all I wanted to do was leave. You have been my support community—even when you did not know it.

Most importantly, I would like to thank my wonderful family members who have plowed through this uncharted ground with me. I would never have started this journey if not for the support of my best friend, prayer partner, and wife, Nancy. She has steadfastly marched by my side through the entire journey and has endured the brunt of my frustrations and stresses while she demonstrated the love of Christ that I can only try to emulate. To my children, Joshua and Hannah, who have sacrificed far too much precious time with their dad; I look forward to making some of that up to both of you.

The final note of gratitude goes to the One who loved me enough to restore my relationship with Him through the death of His Son, Jesus Christ. Truly, without God in my life, there would be no reason to try and pass on some seeds of wisdom to another generation or work to stay in the fight. God alone has kept me from quitting—by reminding me of His promise: "God so loved the world that He gave His one and only Son, that whoever believes in Him shall not perish, but have everlasting life" (John 3:16, NIV). Thank you, Father, for an unbelievable journey.

INTRODUCTION

I looked around the cracked, pale, green-painted cinderblock walls as a window air-conditioner hummed in the background and I was reminded how itinerant ministry is often not what most people expect. Although I had been told not to despise small beginnings during the early years of ministry, the motel room that I found myself in was after several years and many such motels. I have had the privilege of staying in wonderful hotels in extravagant places, but those all seemed far away in a different world from where I was right then.

In that moment of familiarizing myself with a new environment, I made an unconscious decision. At first, I did not even realize that a decision had been made, but afterward I knew that I could have either allowed the enemy room in my heart by becoming upset with my new circumstances, or sense God's desire that I should be thankful for what He had provided. God does have the uncanny ability to keep His servants humble in one way or another while teaching them through the most unconventional methods.

So, I was reminded that I should have an attitude of thankfulness for what had been provided, not remorse at what was lacking. I should be thankful that the church had enough foresight to take care of accommodations the only way they knew how. I should appreciate the fact that I even had a place to preach for the following series of services. And be thankful for a pastor who had enough concern to ensure the expense of this room was taken care of, even though it was a sacrifice. I knew that the pastor did not have a large salary or a huge congregation, but they did have a solid church in the middle of rural America that needed spiritual renewal.

God continues to teach all of us who desire to be life-long students of His Word and His ways, that He always goes before us to prepare the way. Although I will always have much to learn, I pray that the following pages will be helpful in your journey as you step out into one of the most challenging vocations today, that of an evangelist for Jesus Christ.

For Him,

Marshall

CHAPTER 1

Why Evangelists Do What They Do

As I walked up the stairs to the hotel conference room, I wondered what I would find. I had initiated our first Evangelists and Friends Gathering to help encourage and provide fellowship for fellow evangelists and those who believed in the calling of the evangelist. Although the event attendance was small, there was a spark of something that would encourage me in a future meeting the following year. But all I could think about on this day consisted of trying to see what God had in mind when He prompted me to organize this event.

I originally sensed the Lord directing me to start these gatherings because I knew evangelists and their families often lacked opportunities to fellowship and find encouragement. Oftentimes, evangelists are branded as "Lone Ranger" types and usually have limited outlets for deep relationships that could help them in ministry and personal life. I felt these gatherings could also assist young ministers sensing the call to evangelistic ministry through mentoring and joining in some fun activities and just hearing some of the stories that a veteran evangelist might share.

The second day of our first Evangelists and Friends gathering found several evangelists sitting around a table, talking about ministry during our question and answer time. At one point, I asked: "How can we help young evangelists enter ministry today?"

Ironically, after voicing several thoughts that failed to garner much conversation, someone said, "You know, it's really all about the call," meaning that it was really all about God's call to evangelistic ministry.

As we discussed this aspect of evangelistic ministry, the simplicity of that statement rang true like the sound of church bells on a quiet, crystal-clear morning. Even the apostle Paul declared that he was, "a prisoner of Jesus Christ" (Philemon 1:1; 9 KJV). Although mentoring and support systems could improve, along with logistical insights and coaching opportunities, the simple fact remained is that without God's call to evangelistic ministry, no one would ever endure the hardships that face every minister at some point in his or her ministry. Hardships such as the love offerings that barely covered fuel costs to the accommodations that left you asking God why He had forsaken you to the unfriendliness that can meet a guest speaker in a plethora of situations.

Every minister has times when he or she questions the call – but it is the call that keeps every one of us on the Gospel road. Through all the unpleasantness of ministry (and there will be plenty), God will reward your faithfulness and commitment to His Word and His way—a way filled with truth and integrity. When you see someone cross the threshold of faith and become a follower of Christ, you will realize why you do what you do.

A couple of interesting events happened to me when I first began our evangelistic ministry, and they have stayed with me over the years. The first event happened at one of my first services. Our family had ministered in the morning service, but in the evening service the Lord's presence was powerful and ministered to many in attendance as the pastor and I prayed for them. The church was small, and the congregation consisted mainly of senior citizens—one of whom the Lord had truly touched.

After the service had ended, folks came by to shake my hand and thank our family for coming. The elderly lady whom God had touched was being helped to the front of the church by a friend. When she stood in front of me, she said, "Brother Windsor, I don't have much, but I wanted to give you something."

She placed some coins in my hand, and I just thanked her and gave her a hug. I put the coins in my pocket without looking at what she had given me, because I was trying to focus on the people around me at the time. Later, after we left the church, I pulled the coins out of my pocket and showed my wife, Nancy, what this dear saint had given. She had placed four quarters in my hand that night, and I couldn't help but think of the widow's two mites that Jesus talked about in Mark 12:42-43. The Lord truly humbled me and reminded me of her sacrifice that night. I still have those four quarters to remind me that many will give out of their need.

The second event happened after we purchased our first travel trailer. It was a used, fifth wheel recreation vehicle (RV) that I could tow with my pickup truck. We purchased this trailer to help us as we traveled to churches in rural communities where hotels were scarce. The RV would provide lodging as we ministered in churches without the resources available to help with the expense of hotel accommodations for several days during special meetings. We looked forward to the new opportunities that God would open up for us with our newly purchased RV.

Shortly thereafter, I called a pastor and booked some revival services that would require us to bring our RV. I inquired as to whether the church had the appropriate hookups for an RV and the pastor assured me that they did. He said that they did not have sewer or water hookups, but he did have electricity. I felt like we could make this work with the storage capacity of our RV and booked the revival meeting there in August.

When we arrived, I found that his electricity hookup was only a 15-amp, 120-volt outlet on an electric pole some distance from the church. Because it was August, we needed to run our air conditioner unit, but this caused the circuit breaker to trip frequently. This, in turn, caused our RV to feel like an oven. I had to rewire the electric outlet and the pastor graciously purchased the supplies we needed from the local hardware store.

During that week, I preached my heart out, and God touched many people. It was so encouraging to fellowship with the pastor and his family, as well as seeing all that God was doing in the lives of those in attendance. When the revival services ended, the pastor handed me a check for $200 for the entire week. We had spent so much on fuel and food to get there, and we had other bills we needed to take care of and all the pastor gave us was $200. Right then and there I began to question the Lord if He really knew what He was doing or whether we had just missed Him in answering the call to ministry!

To say I was discouraged would be a gross understatement. I loaded our family up in the truck and left to go home—never saying a thing to the pastor. I felt like I should always put on my best face and let God deal with church leaders who treated us unfairly. I had always been told that God would make up the difference, but I was hard-pressed to see that at the time. The following week we had another service that was a Sunday morning only event. The pastor had assured me that they had an "evangelist quarters," or special room in the church for guests, so we left our RV at home.

When we rolled up to the church on Saturday evening, the pastor was there and showed us where we would be sleeping. There were a room and bed for Nancy and me, as well as a bed made up for the kids. On each of the beds sat a food basket filled with all sorts of fruit, snacks, and treats. I had only heard of such gracious hosting before, but to see it after my discouraging week before left me speechless.

The evangelist quarters also had a small kitchen that the church had stocked with plenty of breakfast items, and we were instructed to help ourselves. We were overwhelmed by the church's generosity, and after the one morning service on Sunday the pastor handed us a check for $500. It was as though the Lord was confirming that He, indeed, took care of those who answered His call.

Although these stories are personal references, you can ask almost any evangelist, and they can share similar stories of how God has provided in unimaginable ways. He leads us all through tests and trials, which often seem as dark as a moonless night sky. Yet, He uses all of that to show us His unwavering ability to care for us when we abandon ourselves to His calling. Truly, it is all about the call—that's why evangelists do what they do.

CHAPTER 2

A Little Theology

You must know the biblical basis of your calling if you sense God is calling you into evangelistic ministry of any kind: a full-time vocational evangelist, a bi-vocational evangelist, or a lay person who loves to evangelize. You may have others who ridicule your profession and try to sway you to follow another direction, but if you know your calling is grounded in the Word of God and you have no doubt that God has called you—then you will have established a solid underpinning for your calling and work as an evangelist.

Although there are some individuals calling themselves evangelists, this in itself cannot be the validating foundation of a person's ministry. Fruit will be the unquestionable witness to any ministry, whether it is called of God or man. But because of the plethora of itinerant ministries today, there seems to be vagueness surrounding the role of the evangelist. The New Testament gives us some valuable insights into the role and function of the evangelist, and that is where we must begin.

We see the term "evangelist," as translated from the Greek word *euangelistes*, literally means "bringer of the Gospel."[1] This word also uses the same root as *euangelion*, meaning "gospel" or "good news," as well as *euangelizomai*, meaning to "proclaim" the good news or gospel. The Greek word *euaggelion*, translated gospel, "comes from the word godspell

---

1   Robert M. Abbott, "The Assemblies of God Evangelist Life and Work," (Springfield: Gospel Publishing House, 1988): 7.

– a story about God,"[2] and it is this story about God that all believers are responsible for telling. The word *euaggelizo* for "I preach," is seen fifty-four times in the New Testament, and of the fifty-four occurrences, twenty of those are in participle form signifying a continuous action. The use of the word *euaggelistes* or evangelist is only seen three times in the New Testament: Phillip in Acts 21:8, Paul's description of the gifts in Ephesians 4:11, and Paul's admonition of Timothy to "do the works of an evangelist" in 2 Timothy 4:5.

In biblical times, the evangelist began as a proclaimer of the good news, or gospel, of Jesus Christ and the "evangelist's calling originally denoted both a function and an office."[3] As a matter of fact, the roles of the apostle and evangelist have many similarities, in that "all apostles were evangelists; however, not all evangelists were apostles,"[4] which we can still see today within the church if we look closely. It is not within the scope of this book to argue for the continuation of the office of apostle, but there are many who feel the modern missionary often functions in the calling or parameters of this spiritual ministry gift to the church.

Evangelism announces the good news of Jesus Christ through whatever means, methods, and messengers the Lord so chooses to use. These variables in evangelism can be as diverse as night and day or ice cubes and cucumbers, but we must remember, evangelism cannot be defined in terms of successful results. The New Testament reveals that wherever the good news is proclaimed some will respond with repentance and faith, while others will be indifferent and still others will reject it (*e.g.* Acts 17:32–34; 2 Corinthians 4:3–4).[5] God, Himself, will bring forth the fruit of our labors if we are faithful to our calling. The

---

2   Gordon L. Anderson, "The Evangelist: Winning the Lost – Reviving the Church," *Enrichment*, 4, no. 1 (Winter 1999): 17.

3   James O. Davis, "The New Testament Evangelist and the 21st-Century Church," *Enrichment*, 4 no. 1 (Winter 1999): 13.

4   Ibid.

5   Sinclair B. Ferguson and J.I. Packer, "Evangelist" in *New Dictionary of Theology*. electronic ed. Downers Grove, IL : InterVarsity Press, 2000, c1988, S. 240.

original Greek words pertaining to evangelism pose different challenges to us as we strive to see what the Scriptures teach us about evangelists. The word evangelist and the person of the evangelist have come to mean different things over the centuries since the time of Jesus Christ. There was a limited use of the word in the New Testament times, and we know that Paul told Timothy to "do the work of an evangelist."

Apparently, the word was well known in Paul's day, and this type of lifestyle was common and expected of every Christ-follower. Even Ephesians 4:11-13, the cornerstone and directive of this gifting, says that it is "to prepare God's people for works of service, so that the body of Christ may be built up until we all reach unity in the faith and in the knowledge of the Son of God and become mature, attaining to the whole measure of the fullness of Christ." (NIV)

The word for "service" found in verse 12, *diakonia* in the Greek, can also mean ministry or mission. So, the five-fold ministry gifts of God to His church were for preparing God's people, or "the Holy Ones," for works of service, for works of ministry, for works within the mission of God—bringing people back into a right relationship with Him.

Thus, we see discipleship in action. New believers in Christ were dedicated to a life-long attitude of learning, as well as sharing the good news of Christ with others in hopes that they too would come to a saving knowledge of Jesus Christ, knowledge gained by letting Christ have leadership and lordship over their lives—while receiving the priceless forgiveness of sins.

However, over the centuries we have unfortunately seen the church less committed to discipleship responsibility. Obviously, there are many effective church leaders who have positioned people around them to help strengthen the church's outreach focus. But, in many instances, the demands of our culture have caused the church's focus to become more internal instead of external to provide spiritual leadership to the people who have joined our congregational communities.

In a way, we became maintenance minded. The church began leaning more on the "evangelist" to come in and help win souls for the Kingdom of God. Popularity grew as large crusades not only brought souls into the Kingdom of God, but also acceptance that this was God's only means for helping people find salvation. However, the reality is that "your church will be an outsider-oriented ministry only if you and the other leaders become outsider-oriented leaders."[6] The gift of the evangelist can be a multifaceted resource to help equip church communities for an outsider-oriented focus—especially in today's missional-focused church.

If Jesus is our high priest and example of Christ-like living, then we must note that He shared the Gospel and many followed him. Paul followed Jesus' example. He shared the Gospel message for the first time with the Gentile, Cornelius, and his entire household—of Jesus Christ's acceptance of them. Likewise, we should also share this message with others.

Paul said in Acts 10:37-38, "You know what has happened throughout Judea, beginning in Galilee after the baptism that John preached—how God anointed Jesus of Nazareth with the Holy Spirit and power, and how he went around doing good and healing all who were under the power of the devil, because God was with him." Paul went on to say in verse 39a, "We are witnesses of everything he did in the country of the Jews and in Jerusalem."

Even as Jesus went about doing good, we are all admonished to "go about doing good." As Christians, we should all follow Jesus Christ in doing good to others and being "witnesses of everything He did" in our own lives. But as the church grows and its people become prepared for "works of service," the church itself should become an evangelistic entity within its local community. Even now, we can see the explosion of church planting that has taken place in the United States alone. However, helping new churches—and new believers—become evangelism tools for Christ remains a real need in the church today.

---

6   Mark Mittelberg, *Becoming A Contagious Church*, rev. ed. (Grand Rapids, MI: Zondervan, 2007), 31.

What does that mean for the centuries old gift of the evangelist for the Kingdom of God? The word evangelist literally means a purveyor of the "gospel or good news;" and every Christian is called to share the good news of Jesus Christ. The Lausanne Congress on World Evangelization (1974) agreed to the following statement:

To evangelize is to spread the good news that Jesus Christ died for our sins and was raised from the dead according to the Scriptures, and that as the reigning Lord he now offers the forgiveness of sins and the liberating gift of the Spirit to all who repent and believe. Our Christian presence in the world is indispensable to evangelism, and so is every kind of dialogue whose purpose is to listen sensitively in order to understand. But evangelism itself is the proclamation of the historical, biblical Christ as Savior and Lord, with a view to persuading people to come to him personally and so be reconciled to God. In issuing the gospel invitation, we have no liberty to conceal the cost of discipleship. Jesus calls all who would follow him to deny themselves, take up their cross, and identify themselves with his new community. The results of evangelism include obedience to Christ, incorporation into his church and responsible service in the world.[7]

With communities as large as we have today, every Christian can be an evangelist—a resource to the local church that helps bring others into God's new community of Christ followers. We all have a realm of influence, which includes those people that we touch every day. God wants to use that influence to further His kingdom!

Today's evangelistic ministry remains a gift of God to the church that goes about doing good. Some evangelists have a passion for revival, invoking the gift of the Old Testament prophet in calling God's people back to a right relationship with Him. Some evangelists are truly gifted in helping bring people to a saving knowledge of Jesus Christ. Whether they work with adults, youth, or children, people receive Christ as

---

7   Sinclair B. Ferguson and J.I. Packer, "Evangelist."

their personal savior. Other evangelistic ministries focus more on the supernatural work of healing and deliverance. Evangelists are pursuing the passion God has given them, no matter what specific burden God has sealed within their hearts.

Down through the centuries, for whatever reason, we have tended to see the evangelist as proclaimer and revivalist, with Charles Finney even declaring that revival had two functions: "to win the lost and to revive the church."[8] Gordon Anderson, the president of North Central University, had this to say concerning the role of evangelists:

The evangelist preaches the good news to sinners, makes converts, and baptizes them. That is the primary role of the evangelist. However, there seems to be another role, which is not only preaching salvation to sinners, but also preaching revival to believers.[9]

Although there are arguments whether an itinerant minister is an evangelist or revivalist, one thing is clear: "Evangelists have a dual role; a soul-winning and a strengthening ministry."[10] Within the confines of the New Testament, we see the evangelist not only proclaiming the gospel "in new areas," but also preaching Christ to those who are "saved." Luke 10:1-19 reveals the "Preacher-evangelist," Acts 8 demonstrates the "Power-evangelist," and 2 Timothy 4:5 describes the "Pastor-evangelist."[11] And if one wants to argue about the differing roles of apostle, missionary, and evangelist, we could always remind them that it was the evangelist (Phillip) who told of the first Gentile converts.

Billy Graham said, "Methods may differ according to the evangelist's opportunity and calling, but the central truth remains: an evangelist has been called and specially equipped by God to declare the Gospel to

---

8   Anderson, 18.

9   Ibid.

10 Davis, 14.

11 Ibid.

those who have not accepted it, with the goal of challenging them to turn to Christ in repentance and faith."[12] So in the truest and strictest sense of the word, tradition has helped shape our definition of an evangelist, because the Bible doesn't say anywhere that the evangelist is a soul winner—only someone who proclaims the good news as Dr. Graham stated, with the goal of bringing the hearers to a decision for Jesus Christ.

Today, the evangelist is still a purveyor of the "Good News" of Jesus Christ, but the title "evangelist" has come to include anyone with an "evangelistic lifestyle" who shares the Gospel message through multiple talents and methods. That means they are individuals called of God to a traveling ministry—not just a preaching ministry. They do not reside in any one place, but travel about as opportunities for service, ministry, or mission arise.

Additionally, the evangelist should see himself as a coach and a cheerleader to the local church, helping church leaders with education, healing, encouragement, and exhorting every Christian layperson to share the Gospel message with the lost. The evangelist stands as a model to other young evangelists who are coming up in the church.

When evangelists come to a church, outreach, or other special event and extend a salvation invitation, it seems that more people respond to that invitation for a decision than would normally occur. People that you have been trying to get in your church for years—to no avail—suddenly show up that day and cross the line of faith! It makes you want to say: "Man, I've been working for years to get them to the altar and now this evangelist comes and gets all the credit." Well, God should really be getting all the credit, but sometimes you wonder what was so different! The calling upon that minister's life was different—that is all.

---

12 Billy Graham, *A Biblical Standard for Evangelists* (Minneapolis, MN: World Wide Publications, 1984), 6.

Most itinerant ministers share the Gospel in one form or another, and if the truth were known, every Christian should have a heart for people to come to a saving knowledge of Jesus Christ. I'm classified as an evangelist, and I really try to sense the Holy Spirit's leading in what God wants to do in a particular church setting. If I'm going to a church, I understand that there are many Christians there, but I need to realize that there might be a lost person there too. Additionally, there are probably, more often than not, some people who aren't where they need to be with God and need to have their spiritual relationships strengthened. I want to do everything I can to sense God's direction so that God can minister to everyone who comes to that service.

Evangelists travel from place to place, depending only upon their faith because they depend on other people to support them. They do not have a salary per se unless their ministry has grown into a large, incorporated organization. They will not usually have a monthly salary, but subsist on what each church gives them for travel expenses and honorarium—or love offering as it is often called. Evangelists are folks who may have lots of different methods of ministry: music, drama, feats of strength, or something else that may present itself as relevant in future years. Your imagination is the only limitation to how you can conduct and utilize evangelistic ministry.

Some denominations have established special groups for evangelists who are true soul winners. However, if we pursue that direction, we foster the perception that the "true" evangelist is a soul winner without any other venues of service. The designation of "harvester" evangelists was created to help clarify those evangelists who are true soul winners and those doing something else—as though that was second best.

If someone is going about "doing good" in other ministry emphases as the Holy Spirit has called them to, isn't that laudable? Even Jesus went about healing and using that means to share the power of the Gospel and bring glory to God. He used deliverance as another means to display the good news in action. Can't we use drama, music, and other God-given talents and abilities to "travel about" and share the good news? I think we can. We don't need to use the evangelist "soul-winner-only" mentality to strengthen the misperception that if we want to win souls we need to bring in an "expert."

Labeling an evangelist as a "soul-winner" or "harvester" also seems a bit unbiblical. Paul told the Corinthian church in 1 Corinthians 3:6, "I planted the seed, Apollos watered it, but God made it grow." God alone deserves all glory and praise for any additions to His kingdom, because as Jesus said in John 6:44, "No one can come to me unless the Father who sent me draws him, and I will raise him up at the last day." Titles like soul-winner or harvester are well-intentioned, but perhaps encourage a bit of vanity and will not help anyone gain a step toward Heaven—only the sweet Holy Spirit of God can do that.

Interestingly, the secular, corporate world has its own brand of evangelist, and they are called that—evangelists. Microsoft, IBM, and others have "evangelists" who share the good news of their employers. Previously known as "salesmen," some corporations have now adopted the church's gift of the "evangelist" to add value to what they do. How many of us have wonderful memories when someone mentions the word "salesman"? Not too many of us I would presume.

You can probably recall the car salesperson who wouldn't leave you alone, the water softener salesperson who knocked on your door shortly after you moved into a home, or the luxury condo salesperson who put on the "pressure sales" tactics to get you to sign your name on the dotted line. Pressure, deception, liar, thief, and a myriad of other adjectives just might come to mind when thinking about a salesperson.

But there are literally thousands of God-loving salespeople who are trying to be honest and do things right, sellers of something. Some people could sell ice cubes to those living so far north that ice is never a problem all year round! It is their gifting and talent. But to defuse the negative connotations with the title "salesperson," the corporate world has adopted the term evangelist to associate a more positive perspective on their organization's sales specialists.

So too, in today's church many have moved into a corporate mindset and look for "specialists" who can come alongside and help their congregations with healing, Holy Spirit baptism, family life, or a host of other "specialties" that church leaders need. Although this is an honest approach within the body of Christ, mainly in larger congregations, those churches are not in the majority.

With most churches consisting of less than a hundred people today, many pastors are not looking for a specialist, but a practitioner who knows how to touch Heaven and be led by the Holy Spirit. They need someone who has such sensitivity to the Holy Spirit that they can discern what is needed without anyone telling them—someone who can be a confidant and friend, a counselor, an encourager, and an equipper of the saints for "works of service." People should experience healing, soul winning, and the miraculous in the local church—every day of the week.

God gave the ministry gifts to the Church so that it could grow and bear fruit for the glory of God. He told us: "I am the Lord; that is my name; my glory I will give to no other, nor my praise to carved idols" (Isaiah 42:8 ESV). All the ministry gifts and talents we have are solely to bring glory to the giver of all good gifts—God Himself. Hopefully, our joined efforts will reap exponential rewards in this life and the eternal life to come, so believe in your calling and realize that your ministry gift rests on the Word of God until the Author comes back for His Church!

CHAPTER 3

The Ministry of the Evangelist

As has often been stated, the methods of preaching must change to show the relevance of the Gospel to our generation, but the message must always stay the same. We must remember that it is the supernatural power of the Gospel that changes people's lives and draws them to the Creator of the universe. As the apostle Paul wrote in Romans 1:16 (KJV), the Gospel of Christ "is the power of God unto salvation to everyone that believeth; to the Jew first, and also to the Greek."

Every true vocational and volunteer minister of the Gospel of Jesus Christ is working towards the furtherance of God's kingdom – "For the perfecting of the saints, for the work of the ministry, for the edifying of the body of Christ" (Ephesians 4:12 KJV). That said, we are all called to have the heart of an evangelist and to do the "work of an evangelist" according to the apostle Paul in his letter to Timothy (2 Timothy 4:5). Seeing someone cross the line of faith into a right relationship with God through His son, Jesus Christ, should be the ultimate goal for every Christian.

As supposed by some, but perhaps inaccurately, Saint Francis of Assisi is claimed to have said: "Preach the Gospel at all times and when necessary use words." May we all strive to be so associated with the message of Jesus Christ in the everyday aspects of our lives that people will not have to ask whether we are Christians—much less evangelists.

Concerning evangelists, most itinerant ministries share the Gospel in one form or another, but through differing means. Today, there are evangelists who proclaim the Gospel through music, drama, preaching, and other peculiar ministries. There are itinerant chaplains, or evangelists, who minister to rock climbers, rodeo personnel, motorcycle groups, and a myriad of other specialty groups that one would never have imagined in the days of yesteryear. Some itinerant ministers sense God's special calling to teach on special areas of the Scripture, like spiritual gifts, prophecy, healing, discipleship, and Holy Spirit baptism.

Additionally, more venues than ever before are open for evangelistic ministry. Many school assemblies have invited evangelists in to share motivational messages that often include an invitation to an evening rally where the Gospel is presented. College campuses often have spiritual organizations that may invite an evangelist to minister in special meetings. Horse racing stadiums often have chapel areas where chaplains or special guests can minister to support personnel.

I have had the privilege of working with military chaplains for special services to our military personnel and civilians overseas, as well as with missionaries for teaching, training, and special conferences. When opportunities arise to partner with other spiritual leaders, you must maintain a sensitivity to protocol in that environment and abide by those standards at all costs. Jesus Christ exhorts us all to submit to authority.

Churches with numerous cell, or home groups can have celebration services where guest speakers are invited to bring a special message and foster a sense of unity within all the differing small groups. Ministry groups within a church may also bring in an evangelist for special messages. These ministry groups could include women's ministries, men's ministries, campouts, special camp conferences, ministers' meetings, leadership conferences, marriage retreats, and more.

I remember sharing an evangelistic message with a group of boys who were part of a church campout. It seems like there is something special about sitting around a campfire and sharing what Christ can do in a person's life. Don't be afraid to dream big and see where God will lead you and your ministry of evangelism—proclaiming the message of hope to every corner of the globe.

MINISTRY IN A LOCAL CHURCH SETTING

Church leaders can incorporate evangelists and itinerant ministers into a regular system of exposing their people to the different ministry gifts and teachings of Scripture. No church leader can boast of being great at every biblical gift. God has given these ministry gifts to the church to build up and equip a body of believers who can help proclaim and teach the Gospel message to the farthest reaches of the Earth. It's a team effort!

Additionally, the evangelist can be a great evangelism cheerleader for a congregation and can often share things with a congregation that a pastor might otherwise avoid. The evangelist should be just like a glove on a pastor's hand. Gloves are used when hard work is needed along with a little protection for one's hands. That doesn't mean that you have to act and sound exactly like the pastor does. It means that you should try to model the presentation methods of the pastor—like the version of Scripture used, clothing style worn if you are comfortable with it, and length of sermons.

You are trying to connect with a group of people you do not know and presenting yourself in a fashion similar to the pastor will go a long way in breaking down barriers. That said, don't try to be someone you are not. Authenticity goes a long way when trying to connect with a new congregation. You still need to share whatever God tells you to speak to that group of people, but try to be a glove on the pastor's hand when you say it.

The evangelist or itinerant minister can also teach evangelism and outreach principles to local congregations. This can include merely teaching or the incorporation of outreach teams that literally put into practice what is being taught. Do your planning with the church leaders so that everyone has a part in the communication and planning process. Coordinate teams so that no one person goes out alone. Most outreach teams don't go into homes, but pray or extend invitations at the door.

Regardless of the teaching or outreach functions a church uses an evangelist for, evangelism should be a key part of your discipleship program! As an evangelist, you can help stir outreach creativity with local pastors and assist them in following through on their plans. If you have the gift of teaching, expose others to great teaching resources and demographics to help highlight potential ministry areas within their respective communities.

The evangelist can be used as a motivational or instructional speaker for lay evangelism teams. If a local church already has an evangelism or outreach team, an evangelist can bring some renewed energy, excitement, and challenge to outreach. As an evangelist, you model what an evangelist looks like, sounds like, and acts like. You can be a wonderful catalyst that helps motivate people within the local congregation who may have grown a bit complacent in their witnessing or outreach initiatives. It's always worth the investment in local church evangelism teams to bring in someone who can model and motivate those who can reach a local church's community. Bring witnessing tools and ideas to the table and add value to those precious saints who take the Gospel to their local community every day!

Lastly, the evangelist can be used to help a church's focus on special community events (community services, outreaches, carnivals, all church services, etc.). When there is a special event—like the Fourth of July—a special speaker often brings added excitement and expectation. Try to be a part of that local church's planning with these types of events and be prepared to let pastors or outreach ministers know that it is better to do fewer events with excellence than to do a multitude of mediocre events that leave people wondering why they came.

MINISTRY IN A MISSIONS SETTING

After I had settled into my airplane seat, I opened my cards from Nancy and the kids. I was preparing for two eight-hour flights and was a little depressed because today was my birthday and I was headed to Africa on a mission trip. When I opened a card, I discovered a photo of Nancy, Joshua, and Hannah along with some words of remembrance. Tough? You bet. I'll never forget flying to another country and leaving my family behind for almost two weeks.

But, the first mission trip I took captured my heart and I've never been the same since. Thankfully, over the years, my family has been able to accompany me on most of these trips, but connecting with others in a mission context is a bit different than your local church in America. I share more about actual ministry in an overseas context in Chapter 10, but here are a few lessons I have learned.

One thing you learn early on is that when you've seen one developing country, it seems like you have seen them all. A lack of water, electricity that may be intermittent—if at all—and restroom facilities are only a few of the considerations when ministering abroad. Always pack your bag for worse case scenarios, which means a jar of peanut butter, toilet paper, antibacterial ointment, insect repellent and small packs of trail mix and vitamins.

Ensure visa requirements are met by visiting federal websites and be sure to check on any additional vaccines you may need before traveling. Split your money up and stash it in several places. Always plan for tips ahead of time and have those smaller bills in a pocket that will allow you to simply pull that tip out without showing how much money you may have on your person.

Thieves are rampant overseas—and some places here in America as well! An interesting trick that was played on a friend of mine ended with their camera being stolen. They were in a car driving in an overseas town with lots of traffic. It seems like there is always a lot of traffic! They had their windows down (first mistake) and were creeping along in stop-and-go traffic. Someone bumped the car on one side, and while everyone looked that way, someone else snatched the camera out of my friend's hands from the other side of the car. A tough lesson indeed!

That is why, no matter how many countries you may have been in or plan to conduct ministry in, you need to coordinate your efforts with local missionaries and ministries that may already be working in that area. They will know all about these preemptory safeguards and how best to handle accomplishing ministry goals in that community. They will understand local protocols and traditions that can be sacred. Value their counsel and experience so that you do not have to relearn everything in that ministry context. They will also be able to follow-up and help you hand off successful ministry to those who remain behind.

There are numerous ministry opportunities in foreign countries. In recent years, there has been a large initiative to raise up Bible colleges in developing countries to train leaders who in turn can teach and train those indigenous people how to take the Gospel to their own people. Obviously, people will more readily listen to someone who looks and talks just like they do. Those people also take note of the supernatural, which seems to happen more often in impoverished communities.

Additionally, humanitarian aid and orphanages are tremendous venues for helping others and sharing the love of Jesus Christ. Crusade Evangelism also continues to be effective in developing countries— especially parts of Africa, India, and South America.

With all of these opportunities, you must pray for God's discernment and strive to work with existing missionaries onsite if possible. If you are going to unreached people groups, try to connect with regional leaders who can provide insights into those people and challenges that you may face. Your ministry may grow so that you establish your own ministry office overseas with orphanages or other humanitarian relief initiatives. Work to collaborate with others instead of bringing division and strife.

With God's grace and protection, you will be able to avoid many of the pitfalls that have befallen others, and be part of a great harvest for the Kingdom of God.

SELECTING THE RIGHT EVANGELIST

As you travel, you may be asked by church leaders how they can really find a good evangelist. Because almost everyone has heard a negative story about guests in ministry circles, you need to be prepared to help pastors find quality evangelists who will bless their churches. Following are just a few of the ways a pastor can connect with the right evangelist.

First of all, a leader should be led of the Holy Spirit. No amount of human skill can take the place of actually sensing that gentle nudge by the Holy Spirit when looking for the right evangelist. God knows exactly what a congregation needs and who will best relate to those people. When the Holy Spirit leads a pastor, he or she also has a great defense if they are questioned as to why a certain evangelist was selected over someone else that people in the congregation may already know. Fasting and praying to hear from God are small sacrifices when faced with the possibility of inviting the wrong guest who may have a less than stellar reputation.

Pastors should ask friends and fellow ministers with whom they are acquainted. There is nothing like having first-hand knowledge of a guest from a trusted friend in your ministry circles. They may have experienced a quality evangelist who they can honestly recommend and give you some insights as to what might be expected or needed when they arrive. You might even visit a church nearby where a certain evangelist is ministering in order to witness their ministry in person.

As an evangelist, you can inform church leaders that some organizations have directories of their evangelists. You would be surprised at how many people don't realize the resources that are already available to them at the regional or national levels. The Assemblies of

God maintains an online directory of its evangelists at http://evangelists. ag.org/directory. That directory listing is free for Assemblies of God evangelists and is searchable by name, city, state, ministry emphasis, or district wherein an evangelist resides. You can even search by ministry schedule to see if any evangelists are ministering near you. What a great tool for pastors! The Assemblies of God also provides free websites for their evangelists.

If an evangelist contacts a pastor for ministry, the pastor should request some type of ministry media from them. Listen to these examples of ministry while in a season of prayer to see what God might say about this speaker. Many evangelists have sermons and videos on websites, so make sure to inform pastors they need to visit potential guests' websites and listen or watch their sermon materials. This can also be a great help in seeing how they interact with congregations.

One of the most important things a pastor can do is to check references. I can't tell you how many times I've heard pastors complain about evangelists, yet they never called any of the references that were given. A pastor should always call references because one pastor may not always tell a guest what they honestly think about their ministry. They may not even tell another pastor how they felt about a guest, but there are subtle clues that one can pick up. If a pastor is not truly adamant about you inviting a guest, nor do they have great examples of how that evangelist ministered in their church, you may want to look elsewhere.

As an itinerant minister, you should communicate your needs and encourage a pastor to share his or her expectations for your time together as well. I try to have as few needs as possible because I work hard to be a "low maintenance" guest. For the most part, communication is the key to great relationships and ministry experiences. Obviously, there are exceptions, but fewer than you might imagine. As an evangelist, you may even want to utilize some type of feedback form that helps church leaders send in anonymous feedback about your ministry. Have them send it to your church pastor so that they don't feel it will be going to you personally— you'll have more honest feedback that way and more participation too.

I recently read a short article of an evangelist who often spoke for a certain church, but had recently received a very small honorarium for a special event. The evangelist called back and talked with the pastor—whom he had a good relationship with—and humbly asked why the honorarium was so low. When asked how much it was, the church leader apologized profusely and shared that he had never even looked in the envelope and confessed there had been an error.

The evangelist was extremely anxious about doing this since the majority of itinerant folks take their disappointments to the Lord and never say a word about sensitive subjects like this one. But, this helps us see that open communication with humility in a situation where something is obviously wrong becomes a building block for a stronger relationship with that pastor and the local church. Sometimes, the Lord actually leads us to ask a simple question in humility instead of getting bitter about what someone did or did not do.

Evangelists should help pastors understand that they need to plan ahead because good itinerant ministers and evangelists are often booked far in advance. That doesn't mean that pastors should negate the use of younger evangelists either—whose schedules may not be as full—but it does mean that they should plan ahead and let God guide them. When sufficient time is set aside for planning, then provision can be made for the right speaker, the needed finances, along with the appropriate resources and follow-up materials to ensure a great time of ministry for everyone.

Some leaders feel that because they pastor smaller churches they cannot have quality guest speakers come in to help them. An evangelist should be a strategic resource person to help reveal possible options to solve these problems! One strategic way to help facilitate ministry opportunities is to have a revival or evangelism fund. With something like that in place a church can take a special offering on the fifth Sunday or another special day of the month or quarter.

Faith promise forms can also be used six months to a year ahead of special services to involve the congregation and raise the needed funds.

Faith promise forms allow people to pledge a certain monthly dollar amount "as the Lord provides" above their tithes. It's amazing to hear some of the testimonies about how God worked in people's lives to help them honor their faith promises!

Smaller churches can also partner with larger churches to possibly help with accommodations and/or travel expenses. Maybe a larger church has a special speaker on a Sunday morning or evening, and the smaller church can utilize that same speaker for several services during the week. Some districts even have special funds available for evangelists to come in and help with revitalization and church planting.

Church leaders can read through the booklet, "Pastor's Reference Guide to Utilizing Evangelists and Itinerant Ministries" that is available online. This booklet helps the local pastor realize the importance of evangelists and shares important considerations when bringing in an evangelist, missionary, or any other itinerant minister as a guest. It also has a checklist for events to assist pastors in having a successful time of ministry.

Church leaders should contact their district, region, or national organization for help with specific questions. The Assemblies of God utilize a national evangelist representative who can help with any questions or problems concerning itinerant ministries at (417) 862-2781 ext. 1302 or email at evangelists@ag.org.

USING THE "TRADITIONAL" EVANGELIST AND REVIVALIST

Tradition ushered in an era of brush arbor or camp meetings, then tent meetings and revival meetings that went on for weeks at a time. The old brush arbor meetings were started in the days of western pioneers in America where there were no buildings, so brush and trees were used to build a sheltered place where folks could worship. In the not-too-distant past, pole barns or similar structures were used to hold revival meetings where the power of God fell. The old-time evangelist was bold, brash, and focused on a no-holds-barred type of preaching that focused on the lost. The audience might include mostly Europeans from one country or another and possibly some Native Americans as can be attested to by many of the old missions still in existence.

Today, tent meetings and extended revivals are not predominant here in the United States except for special community outreach activities. However, crusade-style tent meetings are still popular in many developing countries. God still uses this type of ministry where it is most effective so be open to what God wants to do and be willing to use the method He chooses. Some evangelists have become more specialized in certain areas of ministry to help the local church community in its evangelism efforts and discipleship of new believers.

The more specialized ministry needs of our culture and churches have in large part precipitated the emergence of our existing itinerant ministries. Revivalists, who model the Old Testament prophet in calling God's people back to a right relationship with God, are still desired in many places.

However, specialized ministries are more sought after in the larger, more structured churches. Due to this need, some evangelistic ministries find that God uses them in more specific areas of ministry like healing or Holy Spirit baptism for Pentecostals. True evangelists with the gift of helping people move into a right relationship with God have grown fewer, but the office of the evangelist still finds biblical precedent in the Scriptures.

The avenues for ministry also seem to be shifting today in America. This often depends on which area of the United States you live in, with the Bible Belt having the more traditional Sunday morning, Sunday evening, and Wednesday evening services. Sadly, many churches now only have Sunday morning services due to various reasons, but when no one shows up for service, it's hard to pay the utility bills and have the church open.

Many developing countries only have one Sunday morning service, but it can last several hours because most people walk to church—some several hours. So-called experts have provided copious reasons for the decline in Sunday evening or midweek services, but the reality is that only the local pastor knows why they felt led of the Lord to cut back on opportunities to open the doors of God's house to that community.

Many churches are in a plateau condition and are comfortable there while others are eager to experiment with new forms of ministry. Some church leaders have said: "We don't need evangelists to 'blow in, blow up, and blow out,'" while others believe that there is a valid need for evangelists to come alongside pastors and help. As a matter of fact, the idea of partnerships seems to be a growing trend in the local church today.

Some regions encourage a network of evangelists and pastors. One church used an evangelist multiple times a year so that a trusted relationship developed. That same church utilized a month-long series of meetings—not every service—but an ongoing part of the church activities, which helped the evangelist build those types of relationships. Clearly, that evangelist and pastor developed a great relationship whereby the pastor wasn't worried about the evangelist doing something harmful to his congregation.

WHY SHOULD I UTILIZE AN EVANGELISTIC MINISTRY?

There are many reasons for a pastor to have an evangelist and as an itinerant minister, you should familiarize yourself with some of these reasons if asked. You are the one who your pastor friends will listen to when it comes to questions surrounding evangelists. First and foremost, evangelistic ministry is a scriptural gift from God to the church at large. Additionally, having an evangelist can also help reinforce what you are trying to teach your people.

When an evangelist or itinerant minister begins ministering in the gifts of healing, prophecy, or some other spiritual gift during a service or altar call, people take note of the supernatural. Something divine seems to take place when people feel as though God is working through an evangelist or guest speaker to minister to them personally. God can solidify changes that He has already been working on in an individual's life when that happens.

Using an evangelist or itinerant minister with a special ministry can help strengthen a pastor's weak areas of ministry. God has given the five-fold ministry to the church, and we should not feel as though one person can operate in all the gifts God has given to the Church. Many itinerant ministries provide specific areas of emphasis that would help strengthen a church's congregation. Some areas of ministry might include marriage enrichment, healing, Holy Spirit baptism, End Times, and other relevant areas of teaching.

Many evangelists today come in and help train, encourage, and empower a church's people to get out and share the Gospel. The Scriptures support this aspect of evangelistic ministry in Ephesians 4:11-12. All the ministry gifts should help equip the local body for ministry in that community. If a church incorporates cell or home groups as a normal part of their organization, evangelists and itinerant ministers can be part of combined services that help foster cohesion among a church's people, as well as offer a special time of ministry for all.

There is also a current move towards staff evangelists in many local churches, which seems to be extremely effective. The staff evangelist is an outwardly-focused person who receives an umbrella of protection and accountability from the local church for themselves as well as their evangelistic ministry while helping teach, train, and lead the local church in evangelism and outreach events. It's a win-win situation. They may receive compensation in the way of an office, insurance, or stipend of some sort for their part-time status at the church.

A staff evangelist also helps the congregation and pastor understand the needs of guest speakers and can help facilitate a great outreach ministry experience for the local church. The staff evangelist is a growing position today, in large part because it pays for itself through new converts. These positions are usually part time wherein responsibilities may require one or two weeks out of the month dedicated to church-related training and evangelism. The staff evangelist is allowed to travel some, which helps maintain an awareness of current issues that other churches face in their ministries. He or she is outward-focused, which frees up the pastor to take care of the people that God has entrusted to him or her.

Since compassion ministries seem more effective in reaching people with a spiritual message today, staff evangelists can help teach, train, and conduct church "outreaches," or evangelistic rallies and services that incorporate some aspect of compassion ministry. It is not a "come and see" world anymore. We cannot wait for people to come into our churches to hear the Gospel, but we can utilize evangelistic ministries to help teach, train, and lead evangelism initiatives, as well as deliver timely messages for those within the walls of the church. Many local businesses give resources to these types of ministry because they are helping their own community.

Finally, staff evangelists can spearhead the development of, and ministry to, evangelism teams. These teams will need encouragement at times so church leaders should plan on events that allow for motivational speakers who can speak into the lives of a church's evangelism team. These teams also need recognition in front of the entire church body to be successful, along with celebration services to recognize outreach events that have occurred.

Outside evangelists and other motivational speakers are great at helping in this area. Staff evangelists will be familiar with other itinerant ministries that can complement their and their pastor's ministry. They also understand the issues surrounding itinerant ministries and make wonderful liaisons for the pastor and other staff (i.e. youth, young adult, children's ministry, etc.).

HOW CAN A NATIONAL OFFICE HELP?

Over the years I've sensed that most pastors just want the freedom to hear from God and pastor the church that He has given them. But national organizations have resources that can help the evangelist and local pastor, so why not pray about utilizing those resources? As an evangelist, you should make a point to find resources that can help a local pastor. Anyone that can add value to a local congregation will be seen as an asset instead of a liability. Obviously, the greatest thing you can bring is the Holy Spirit in your own life. Below are some ways a national office might be able to help a local church within the area of evangelism.

National organizations can teach seminars on building an evangelism team, highlight the state of evangelism today on a national level, share insights for effective evangelism they have gleaned from others, reveal some hindrances to the spiritual harvest, share insights for healthy pastor-evangelist relationships, and bring insights on some good evangelism resources. They can also teach on how to ensure you get a "good" evangelistic ministry, and how to get rid of bad ones.

They promote evangelistic ministry and encourage pastors not to give up on evangelistic ministries. If you ever broke your arm, you wouldn't want to do it again. When a pastor has a bad evangelist, the tendency is to never have one again. But, just using "pastor" friends is not rounding out the weaknesses of a pastor's ministry—it's just putting a patch on his or her fears.

A national office can also provide answers to sometimes difficult questions concerning itinerant ministries, helping remove uncertainties associated with having a guest speaker. They often provide a website hub of information and resources for pastors and evangelists and provide feedback opportunities to help bring accountability back into the ranks of the evangelist. National offices usually have an online directory of evangelist contact information, which also serves as a great venue to check up on evangelists referred to you by others. Many evangelists also have personal websites where extra information can be found.

IN SUMMARY

The ministry of the evangelist is something that you have a hard time explaining—primarily because it's about the call of God upon your life. The avenues of ministry have certainly changed over the centuries, but the message continues to be one of hope in the name of Jesus Christ our Lord. As an evangelical evangelist, you have sensed the calling of God that is without repentance (Romans 11:29). It won't let you go, and you cannot run from it—because a calling must be answered. You will never be happy until you yield to God in His pursuit of your life.

Every minister of the Gospel has given up all else for the Kingdom of God. We long to hear the Father say, "well done, thou good and faithful servant" (Matthew 25:21) during the course of our ministry. But whether we hear audibly or not, we must yield to the call. The sacrifices crush us at times and brokenness often meets us at every turn. Yet, to see one born into the Kingdom of God by accepting Jesus Christ as Lord and Savior reminds us all that the sacrifices are worth it.

Today, we seem to be in an era of even more rapid change than ever before. That's why we need evangelists who are empowered by the Holy Spirit of Almighty God. Though some feel the usefulness of the evangelist has passed, the Scriptures dictate otherwise, and interestingly, God continues to call men and women to this challenging area of ministry. Our creativity seems to be the only limitation to ministry in today's ever-changing culture. From Los Angeles to New York, Singapore to London, Bangladesh to Cairo, and Cape Town to Moscow, people need the Lord.

God continues to open new venues of ministry and opportunities for the expansion of His Church and the fulfillment of the Great Commission (Matthew 28:18-20). From social media ministry to staff evangelists, the opportunities for ministry are greater than ever before. Whatever your calling in ministry, do it with the same passion and love we all share for our Heavenly Father: with all your heart, with all your soul, and with all your mind (Matthew 22:37).

CHAPTER 4

The Pastor - Evangelist Relationship

I remember once when I was out in the bush, or a remote village, of Nigeria to preach. We had a great time in the services with about twenty people making salvation decisions. But, after the service they wanted us to go over to the pastor's house, which was a big compliment there. They didn't have a big meal, and as a matter of fact, they didn't even have any meat. We had big slices of bread and French fries. They call them palm frites, or chips, and they weren't necessarily cooked the way I would cook French fries. They were cooked until they were limp and some of them were still a little raw and crunchy.

But, they had somehow purchased a new bottle of ketchup. Now, you need to remember that this is a village where they have thatched roofs and mud walls or concrete, and they had a brand-new bottle of ketchup! They had a big show to make sure that I got to use the ketchup first, which was about as humbling an experience as I have ever encountered. I only had about 5 minutes to eat, because we needed to get back for another appointment with the local missionary. We were really late and trying to hurry to get back before my plane left to return to the United States that day after our appointment.

So, I'm trying to eat and be courteous. It was a huge mound of potatoes, and I just couldn't eat them all. I was praying the whole time that it wasn't insensitive if I did not eat everything they put in front of me. They had sacrificed just to have that brand-new bottle of ketchup.

As evangelists, if we are not careful, we can oftentimes be insensitive to the sacrifices of others where God has opened a door of ministry. That is why it is so important to maintain an attitude of gratitude and remember that our boss never held himself above the people he came to serve. We must be sensitive to the leading of the Holy Spirit as He empowers us to conduct ministry that would be pleasing and glorifying to God. That said, we can learn a lot about fostering a great pastor-evangelist relationship if we'll just take time to model Jesus' example and exercise some common sense with a servant attitude.

BE A GREAT GUEST

Courteous

You need to focus on being a great guest because it is vital to your ministry and being courteous stands as one of the most important qualities of a great guest. You need to treat other people the way that you want to be treated. Show your appreciation for accommodations and the kind of food you receive. You just don't realize the sacrifice the pastor may have had to go through just to provide the room you have and the meals you eat.

In one place, not too long ago, I walked into my hotel room and noticed that the door was really flimsy. It was an old room with an equally old window air conditioner unit and surrounded by painted, concrete walls. I thought: "Oh my goodness." But in that instant, the Lord really helped me make a decision that I could either be bitter, disappointed, or critical of the accommodations that I had been given or I could praise the Lord for the opportunity to minister. I could resent the room provided or be thankful that the pastor was considerate enough to at least provide lodging and food to eat even though it was not what I might have liked.

We must remember that we're servants of the Lord. Also, along those lines, we don't need to be a glutton when they do take us out to dinner. You never order the most expensive item on the menu! If you take yourself out for something to eat by all means order whatever you desire and can afford. But, if someone else is treating you to a meal there is a good rule of thumb to follow for protocol, also called etiquette or manners. Let me share it with you.

Quite simply, this means that you do whatever the host is doing, and however they eat, follow their example. If you're not real sure about those kinds of things, then observe what others are doing and then follow them—especially your host or hostess. Even Proverbs 23:2 (NIV) states: "and put a knife to your throat if you are given to gluttony." Don't be seen as a glutton and taking advantage of other people.

Evangelists need to be good stewards and sensitive while maintaining a servant's heart. This will help us foster a trusted relationship with church leaders where we minister. It takes a lot of hard work to build trust with a pastor and his or her church community. Once you have established that trust, don't abuse it. Being courteous is a vital key to building that trusted relationship and being a good guest.

Communicate

Evangelists obviously need to be good communicators and maintaining good communications with pastors includes sending ministry materials in a timely manner. When you are offered a service opportunity, you need to send a confirmation letter, which helps ensure you are on their calendar. Once you send your confirmation letter, you need to send any ministry promotional materials at least a month prior to your service or series of services.

If you have a little poster or something, send a little note saying: "Hey, we're looking forward to being with you!" You want to do this a month before your service date. Two to three weeks before the service date you should give them a call and say: "I just wanted to check in with you to make sure everything is on schedule for the upcoming services and that we're still planning…" You just need to confirm all those things that pertain to the upcoming service.

When you're talking with the pastor or church contact, there are several questions you should ask. Let me share briefly here some areas you should consider chatting about, and there are further considerations discussed in Chapter 5 as you prepare for actual ministry. Make sure you get directions on how to get to the church. You should also ask the pastor what version of Scripture they use. An evangelist should model a church's pastor so that we can come in and connect with the people as quickly as possible.

One of the ways we do that is to use the same version of scripture the pastor does and use the same sermon timeframe he does—be sensitive to the time. How does he dress? What dress code does he or she normally follow for Sunday morning? Sunday night? The services during the week? Is it ok to dress casual? Can I wear a soft collar shirt? A pullover shirt with a sports coat? What's normative for that church?

You do all of these things through communication—verbal and written. When you get on-site you need to talk over the service, the night before if at all possible. You need to talk about the flow of the service prior to even being there. Ask if it's ok to have a product table? If there's something that you feel the Lord has impressed upon you and it's not what they normally do, then you need to make sure you get permission from the pastor. You need to get a pastor's blessing on what you're doing whether it's a product table or whether you're going to announce the resources that you have.

I always tell people that it's better to let the pastor promote your product table than you because it's just going to detract from the service and the flow of the Holy Spirit if you start promoting things. So, if you are going to promote something, make it really quick, a minute or two and then you need to get on to the service.

Communication is also vital if you have a product table. Visit with the pastor if you need help at the product table. Sometimes churches will provide a person to take care of your table for you if you're not able to be there. However, you need to get the pastors permission beforehand. The last thing you want is to earn the reputation as an evangelist who runs back to their product table instead of ministering to the people during the altar service.

If you have special music visit with the pastor and the worship leader: Is it okay to have special music? Where are you going to perform in the service? How are you going to present it to the congregation? Ask if they are recording the service? If they are, is it possible to get the master so you can offer copies of your ministry to the people at the close of series of services? You should also consider the legal considerations if any music you share is not your own.

Sadly, there are some churches that don't even have sound systems. You don't want to embarrass the leadership of the church by what they don't have, so be sensitive to that possibility. You're there to be a blessing to the pastor and that church body. So, you could ask them: "Do you normally record the services? Do you have a sound system to record the services?" If they don't, you might say: "Hey, that's fine. I always like to check, because if you do, then I'd love to get the masters from you to make copies for the church and to offer to the people as a series at the end of our time with you if that's alright."

There are some evangelists that carry their own sound equipment. Some carry a little portable CD player or other digital recorder, or they may provide an entire sound and video system setup. This is especially true in crusade settings wherein you must provide everything. Some church leaders may say: "Sure, we record video." But it may be a home, hand-held recorder, which won't be very high quality.

So, you need to ask. Because if the pastor says yes, then you're going to have to evaluate it and ask yourself: "Is this a quality recording to reproduce for my product table later on, or for a possible podcast?"

If the recording is just for that local church, they may be used to getting those types of copies. But as far as using those in-house recordings for your own product table, you may need to wait for those churches that have some high-quality equipment and save the master copies for future use.

I've also enjoyed ministry in some churches that have delayed TV programs. I tend to shy away from live television, but the delayed viewing is nice because the church usually has an individual or team that can make edits if needed and then package the video content for television viewing. You have a time window when you need to close, and you must be sensitive to the time if you are recording. Often, the churches that do record will have pretty stringent timelines in the morning. The evening service is usually more flexible where you can minister or do whatever the Lord leads you to do. Communication is just a key to avoiding any misunderstandings and developing life-long relationships.

Confidential

One crucial area of ministry for the evangelist is the role of confidant and friend. You are an encourager for the pastor, his or her spouse, and children. You may see a pastor's children at other major organizational events, and you should make it a point to take them under your wing if possible. Be someone they can call if they need help while in your area or just need someone to talk to or with whom they can pray about sensitive challenges in their lives. Trust takes a lifetime to earn and can be lost in a moment. Be the kind of evangelist who models integrity and attracts people who need a trustworthy friend.

You must keep conversations confidential; and be a confidante for church leaders, because you will hear anything and everything. Far too often, you are the only fellowship that the pastor and their spouse will have had for any extended period of time. It is sad, but many times—especially in small churches—the church leadership can't confide in the church body. So, you're there to minister to the church leaders as well.

A pastor is the entrusted leader of a congregation; so, he or she can't really bear all the church's problems and then share those problems with anyone in the congregation. Usually, with itinerant ministry, 75% or more of your ministry involves ministering to the church leadership, their families, and their children.

As evangelists, we love to talk, but when you find yourself in a setting of personal or problem sharing, you need to learn how to listen. You need to talk less and listen more. Early in ministry, I used to talk all the time to the point of helping other people finish their sentences! Thankfully, with my wife's help, I have worked to be more of a listener than a talker during times of fellowship. Ask questions with a gentle spirit. How can we be praying for you? How can I help you? How are your children doing? What is your biggest challenge right now?

If the opportunity arises, you need to be sensitive because you're trying to develop a relationship that will last. It's not just an opportunity for you to speak and get paid; it's an opportunity for you to gain a friend and a relationship that will last a lifetime. So, we must hone our listening skills as we fellowship—it's all just part of being a great guest.

BE A GIVER

Garnish Others

As a giver, you try to garnish others. That means you try to give and help others by sowing into their ministry. Many times, those in evangelistic ministry love to bless other people because they love to give. We need to be unselfish and generous because it's not all about us; it's about Jesus and it's about being a blessing—not a burden—to the people for whom we minister. If you're a burden, who wants to have you back?

That's also why we need to make sure we're guarding our devotional and study time with God. You can't feed anybody else if you're empty and you must realize that it's the infilling empowerment of the Holy

Spirit that makes our ministries and us effective. It's been said that you can't tell anybody about somebody you don't know. We must do our part to make sure we're spiritually fed and spiritually full; that we're fasting and praying for spiritual nourishment.

Another consideration in garnishing others is that we not manipulate other people. There are a lot of horror stories that church leaders have shared about guest speakers who will come in and begin to manipulate their people for financial gain or ministry results. That really upsets almost everybody involved in that church. We don't need to manipulate pastors or people in the pews during altar invitations, or during the offering time by trying to condemn people for what they can or can't give.

We need to let God be in charge of those things and let God confirm the ministry that He has called us to embrace. God will bear witness to honest ministry conducted with integrity and sincerity. It's been said that money follows ministry and ministry makes room for itself, so focus on God and refuse to adopt some of the shameful tactics that have crept into the Church for financial gain and so-called ministry effectiveness.

If the Lord has really anointed your ministry, then he's going to provide the funds needed to move the ministry along and he's going to open doors of ministry. Who doesn't want to see the miraculous happen or the sick healed or souls being saved or people coming into the Kingdom of God? A Spirit-empowered ministry doesn't need gimmicks or manipulation to appear effective. The word will get out about a ministry that is anointed of the Lord, so we just need to focus on being where God wants us by being led of the Holy Spirit.

In garnishing others, there may be times when pastors or leadership staffs really bless you or they go above and beyond the call of ministry for you. It is very appropriate to send some flowers to them. Perhaps, before you leave town, get some flowers or something and take it by the church or just have the flower shop deliver them. It's always cheaper—even if you're traveling and you don't have time to get them on your way out of town—to place orders at local florist shops over the phone instead of ordering flowers online where it will cost you more.

Call that local florist and have them deliver some flowers to the church. You can find something nice for a reasonable amount of money. Additionally, if it's a smaller, or tight-knit community, you may just generate some positive conversation in town about that church and its guest speaker.

I seem to always think about gift ideas that are cheap or free! When I travel to churches, I'm always on the lookout for books on sale or clearance and I may buy more than one of something when I find a sale. Sometimes when you go to big conferences, they'll have a lot of book giveaways in your gift bags. I'm also always on the lookout for the clearance row. If I can get a book for a couple bucks, then I have something worthwhile to pass on to a church leader. I try to get something that's quality, and I think we need to really be selective in what we provide to the Body of Christ through our ministries.

There are some people that state: "Hey, you need to give a gift at the end of the year to all of the churches you've been to!" But for many churches, that's just a turn-off. They really want something to be from the heart such as a personal letter or a handwritten note or something that would speak a lot louder than buying a trinket or gift. There have been times that I've been impressed to get a nice bookmark or something for people who supported our ministry and wrote a note as well to say thank you and let them know we appreciate them. You just try to be sincere and let people know that you appreciate them as well as the opportunity for ministry. You don't take those opportunities for granted. That's why you need to be selective in your gift giving.

When I bring a book or CD to a pastor, I'll say, "Hey, I just had this little something that I wanted to give to you. I didn't know whether you already had this. If you do, then maybe you know somebody who would be blessed by it." So, I give it as a gift and share: "I just wanted you to know that I was thinking about you and I appreciate the opportunity to be here." I'm always trying to be a blessing to other people and work to garnish others.

Some people on their product table will carry necklaces and bracelets and rings and all matter of stuff. It's one thing to have a t-shirt with a ministry message on it—your ministry tapes or quality books that will really minister to folks. But, all the fashion wear and apparel seem a bit excessive to me. Some people have a mug when they're doing well enough with their logo and their ministry name on it. That's all well and good as a reminder to pray for your ministry. Still, you really need the Lord to guide you in what's going to be tasteful.

Garner As You Go

During ministry, you try to garnish and bless others, but you also need to garner spiritual nourishment for yourself—it takes work to feed yourself. You're going to try to glean insight and wisdom from multiple sources. That's why you never look down on the people you're sent to serve because they can speak into your life just as much as a big conference. One older man who owned a junkyard once shared with me a nugget of truth that the Lord had shown him: "If the devil can't get you sinning, he'll get you busy." I've never forgotten that bit of wisdom that was shared by someone in rural America.

People who have had hard times and lived in the trenches of life can help remind you of God's mercy and grace in your own life and keep you humble. There are many folks who are really destitute—even in America. We can travel to places that are not too far away where people don't have a meal tonight and who don't have very nice clothes to wear. They're struggling. We don't need to look down at them because nine times out of ten they can perceive whether we have a wrong attitude towards them.

Garnering a right spirit allows us the privilege of ministry to these folks who need Christ. It's hard to minister to folks who you cannot relate to or, more importantly, who do not feel that you can relate to them. We really must maintain a servant attitude to truly be effective in ministry and one way we do that is to garner spiritual nourishment for ourselves. It will hone the spiritual blade and keep us spiritually sharp.

Humility will also help us be transparent and let others speak into our lives. However, we shouldn't overwhelm people with our problems. We're there to minister. It's one thing to have a prayer partner or somebody that you can share your problems and concerns with, but don't unload all your hardships on somebody else to whom you're supposed to minister. You're there for them. It's one thing to share a similar story to reveal that you know where they are coming from, but don't share hardship stories to gain sympathy or use as a manipulation tactic.

Using others for personal gain reflects depravity at its lowest level, so don't play on other people's sympathies. If you are not careful, you may begin to share sad stories from the pulpit in order to play on people's emotions. We do care. We have compassion. But, when you play on other people's sympathies you're manipulating them into doing something for you that they wouldn't normally do. We need to let God be our source.

Additionally, we don't need to seek out someone who is affluent in the congregation and work at building a relationship with them so that we can tell them our hardships in order to persuade them into giving us something. That is manipulation, and you're playing on their sympathies. In short, you condemn others through your subtle tactics and work to instill a sense of guilt—that's not God. If you're really spiritual, then you'll pledge to give when asking others to commit to something.

Even during altar calls, fight against using manipulation tactics, but allow the convicting power of the Holy Spirit to move in people's lives. Then, change will be from God and those responding from God's conviction, and leading will undoubtedly be changed for the glory of God. They will have a genuine salvation encounter with their Creator.

What if you have a sermon and there's an illustration that supposedly has an effective impact on your listeners, but it's not for personal gains? Is that permissible? Well, it's one thing to share a personal sympathy story to convey a point in order for people to come to the saving knowledge of the Lord Jesus Christ. In that situation, you are trying to tear down every wall of resistance so that the lost will come and accept

Jesus Christ as the rightful leader and lord of their lives. But, when you use those emotions and sympathies in other people for personal gain and promotion—that is fraudulent and inappropriate. We need to be Holy Spirit empowered men and women of God, full of integrity, who let God really be God in our lives.

In order to garner yourself and garnish others, you should gather gifts as opportunities arise. We previously mentioned this briefly, but you can often find free books from giveaways and conferences, as well as take advantage of publisher discounts when they are present. Some evangelists will visit the different publishing company websites in order to find discontinued items or things that are on sale. These may be quality books that have some age to them. But remember, it doesn't have to be expensive if it's from the heart. Most evangelists don't have much of anything when they first begin in ministry. But, as the Lord provides opportunities, you will find those special deals that help you sow into your life, as well as the lives of others.

End of the year sales are a great way to pick up some inexpensive gifts—especially with publishers. You can even call them and let them know that you're looking for gifts for ministers. They might have some discontinued items with great discounts that you might be able to afford as a pastoral gift or even to add to your own personal library. Many pastors can't afford extra resources like books—even if they are a bit dated—and those gifts are appreciated. As I shared before, if they already have that gift they can pass it on. So, we need to garner as we go. We're garnering to help build and strengthen our walk with the Lord and strengthen the ministry so we, in turn, can give out and garnish others.

Be A Great Gift

The interesting thing about a gift is that it's often a surprise. Most people don't know that they're going to receive a gift—and when God shows up, that's a pretty awesome present. As a matter of fact, being full of the Holy Spirit of God is the best gift we could give anyone as an evangelist. When you are full of the Holy Spirit, your capacity for ministry to others grows exponentially!

Not only is a gift a surprise, but it's also uplifting. From the time that we arrive to the time, we leave we should be people who bless that local church and pastor. We need to be agents of encouragement. We're coaches, cheerleaders, prayer partners, and accountability partners. But most importantly, we need to be uplifting and be a blessing.

A gift should also be edifying. We must be biblical when teaching and preaching God's Word. Don't just tell stories while you're in the pulpit. I so appreciate those ministers who have traveled down the road a lot farther than I have. Their stories are often humorous, enlightening, and biblical. But occasionally, someone will just tell story after story after story without ever quoting or referring to a verse of Scripture. It's the Word of God that will stand the test of time and change lives after everything else is gone.

We also need to be relevant if we want to edify anyone. I read that evangelist Billy Graham would often buy a local newspaper in the city wherein he was ministering to read about local news and events. When we go into new communities, perhaps we need to research local government or news media websites. Buy a local newspaper and find out what's going on in the town. Ask the local Wal-Mart cashier, grocery store clerk, or restaurant waitress: "Hey, what's happening in town this week? Anything exciting going on?" That way you can find out what issues the community might be dealing with and write sermons that are relevant to current issues.

A critical point to remember: A gift doesn't hang around unwanted. Sadly, I heard one story of an evangelist who was blessed financially by a church and all of a sudden, he wanted to move to that city. He wanted to transplant his whole family and be a part of that home church. There were some people in the church who had blessed him and had given him individual offerings as well. They became his best friends! The pastor had to set him down and let him know that it was time to leave. He was no longer a blessing. My pastor friend said, "I'll never have him back."

Those kinds of reports spread like wildfire in ministry circles. You may have gleaned some extra monies in that scenario, but you will destroy your ministry in the long run. You may have extorted—and yes, that's the word I meant to use—money from that one meeting or from those people in a particular church; but you have destroyed a relationship. That relationship could have been a bridge to help you connect not only with that pastor, but also to all the people that pastor knew. So, remember, we need to focus on being a gift and a blessing. Keeping our eyes on the Lord remains the greatest safeguard to being a blessing to other people and the kind of gift that a pastor desires to minister in his or her pulpit.

Receiving Monetary Gifts

What should you do about honest gifts from folks in the congregation or people within the congregation who want to help support your ministry? First, you should always confer with the pastor of that church on what has transpired at some point. Your transparency will alleviate any fears that you are just trying to fleece his or her congregants, so seek God's leading on when and how to share these inquiries about ministry support or personal gifts. This will only solidify your efforts to be a great gift to that local pastor.

One advantage of nonprofit corporation status is that when people in a church want to give specifically to your ministry, they can receive tax deductions. Normal gifts during your services will flow through the churches financial system. However, there are times when people want to give you what they call a Pentecostal Handshake in Pentecostal circles—someone discreetly puts cash in your hand via the guise of shaking your hand. They don't want a receipt; they just want to bless you and your ministry. I usually always tell the pastor what I've been given.

Sadly, I had an evangelist friend tell me one time that a pastor deducted the personal gift given to them from their honorarium. In order to circumvent that, if you are given those kinds of gifts from the individuals, then you could just wait until after the church has given you a gift or honorarium and say, I just wanted to let you know these folks gave me some funds as well. Almost every pastor that I've talked to has said something to the effect: "Hey that's yours. That's between you and them. That's not a big deal." But that's just another reason why we should all be led of the Holy Spirit when dealing with financial issues. The Lord can help us avoid unkind experiences where monies are concerned.

Since the pastor is normally the last person you see before you leave, you should be able to talk about this discreetly. If the pastor is not present, or they had to leave for some unexpected reason, somebody else may take you out to eat afterward or give you the honorarium. When this happens, you might pray about calling the pastor at some point that next week and say: "I just want to thank you so much for the opportunity to minister and the church's financial blessing. I also wanted you to know that so-and-so gave me a little gift." It's not something that you have to feel bad about if you forget to do this or don't have a chance to do it, but I just try to make it an accountability issue for me. I want to make sure that I let the pastor know what's going on.

I don't personally feel like this is a breach of confidence by telling the pastor about my Pentecostal handshakes. If it causes offense, I would be more likely to give the cash back than try to do something behind the pastor's back. You're just appreciative of that gift, and you want to celebrate with the giver as well as the pastor—all while praising the Lord for His goodness. Many times, when people—especially elderly folks— bless my kids, I won't even know about it until after the service and we're on our way down the road. They didn't say anything during the service because I was busy trying to meet people and shake hands. But if you have the opportunity, it's nice to share that with the pastor at some point.

Handling Sensitive Issues

I also make a special effort to chat with the pastor when somebody confides in me about some negative issues in the church. You can usually tell when someone is just trying to cause trouble, and it will mean a lot if you convey this back to the pastor. You want to be seen as the number one advocate for the pastor! I always talk positively about the pastor because I realize they often carry a heavy burden for that local congregation and may have difficult issues they are facing. That's why it's so important to continually work on building trusted relationships with pastors—especially when you are with them for special services.

You should also try to communicate notable altar responses to the pastor if possible. Sometimes people respond to the altar call in a special way. Perhaps they will raise their hand that they need to get right with the Lord or need salvation, but they don't come forward when the invitation is given. I always try to make sure that I let the pastor know—particularly if it's a smaller church and there are only one or two significant responses. Let him or her know who it was who raised their hands for something. You're just trying to be sensitive, a blessing, and a help to the pastor.

Additionally, some people may want to contribute a special offering to your ministry. When a person says: "I would like to make a donation towards a new vehicle, a special outreach/crusade event, or other ministry projects," you would supply them with the proper documentation in order for them to receive giving credit to your ministry. This scenario is not altogether unusual. A person truly feels burdened to help you with certain projects or expenses associated with your ministry.

However, you must keep yourself accountable; and it's a good idea to share this with the pastor. But if the money's going for a specific project like a vehicle, then it should not take the place of an honorarium, which is going to feed you and take care of your fuel to go to the next place of ministry. Normally, you should ask a giver if they want the church to process that special project gift. Then, if you are not incorporated as a nonprofit, they can still get tax-deductible credit. You should always talk about these things with the pastor because they may already have processes in place to help facilitate special offerings.

PASTORS' SURVEY OF EVANGELISTS

I completed a 2006 survey with Assemblies of God pastors concerning evangelists and compared it with a previous one completed in 1996 by Dr. James O. Davis, the Assemblies of God National Evangelist Representative at the time. I asked some similar questions to try and get a comparison over the ten-year span of time, but I also asked some different questions for additional insights. Dr. Davis talked about what "the main qualities looked for in the evangelist" in 1996. Integrity ranked first with 80.6%; solid Bible Preacher was second with 70.1%, and fruitful ministry was third with 60.2%.

Interestingly, more people in 2006 looked for evangelists with integrity! It was still first, but it increased by almost 6%. Solid Bible preacher was still second, but it leaped to 85.1%! I must admit that I was not surprised that servant-hood and humility ranked high. As a matter of fact, it ranked third among pastors with over 73% ranking its importance. One stigma that has probably been rightly earned in the evangelistic ranks is arrogance.

Evangelists get prideful and arrogant being in the spotlight with people looking up to them and praising them all the time. One person shared that evangelists get in trouble when they start believing their own promotional material. If this weren't so true, it would be humorous. Evangelists must work to keep a servant attitude with humility—that's what pastors and lay persons' desire in a minister of the Gospel.

The second question asked if "you hosted a campaign within the last year?" Thankfully, 80.6% said yes and only 19.4% said no in the 1996 survey. Although this specific question was not asked in the 2006 survey, question three revealed that this percentage declined since only 65.3% stated they had a successful campaign in the last 2-3 years.

The successfulness of campaigns was addressed more in questions three and four. In sharing "why was your campaign successful," we had several different responses with 60.7% having success because of souls saved, Holy Spirit baptisms ranked second with 48.5%, and dynamic preaching was third with 47.7% of pastors in the 1996 survey. In contrast, the 2006 survey revealed that the number of souls saved was still number one, but it had fallen to 47.6% by pastors. That should be a very large caution flag waving to all of us in ministry.

Having "personal needs met" was another option added for question four of the 2006 survey. Surprisingly, pastors felt this was very important in the success of a campaign, or evangelist speaker, attested by 46.4% of pastors selecting this response over Holy Spirit Baptisms! That tells me we are entering an era of revival; and also, reveals the need for revival in the local church. The global Church still needs the evangelist who will go out and preach mainly to the lost, but it appears that spiritual renewal is also a vital need.

The global community today has churches with people who need healings, revival, spiritual refreshment, Holy Spirit baptisms, deliverances, and encouragement—they need their personal needs met. With Holy Spirit baptisms falling to a ranking of third behind personal needs met, pastors are saying that revival and revivalists are very important to them.

Question five revealed that pastors no longer invite evangelists into their churches as often when comparing the 1996 and 2006 surveys. Only one-third of pastors surveyed invited evangelists for special meetings once a year and about one-third had two or more meetings a year. Sadly, almost one-third had less than one special meeting a year.

Although the 2006 question is worded slightly different from the 1996 survey, one can see that pastors have moved from having multiple evangelists in a year to some having none at all. The 1996 survey showed 87.9% of pastors hosting one to three meetings a year, while the 2006 survey shows a combined 37.1% and 31.9% of pastors inviting an evangelist at least once a year.

The mega-church complex may have a part to play in this since mega-church pastors, who have more of a corporate mindset, write most of the church growth books today. However, in the Pentecostal arena, a desire for more specialized ministry gifts has emerged in larger churches, which implies that an evangelist who can only preach isn't necessarily desired.

Megachurches often have a staff of pastors or a preaching team, which may negate the sense of evangelistic need. These churches often want a specialized emphasis like family health, baptism in the Holy Spirit, healing, or deliverance. They're moving away from the evangelist with a salvation message because in a larger church venue the pastoral staff may already lead a ministry that performs this task. However, church leaders should prayerfully consider including someone with the evangelist gift—no matter how large the church.

Question six asked what the greatest challenge was for a pastor when inviting evangelists in the 1996 survey, and with long meetings in the 2006 survey. These questions seem to complement one another. In 1996, 54.7% of pastors believed getting the right evangelist was the most challenging problem, 37% mentioned attendance, and 8.3% thought finances were the most challenging. It's interesting that the challenges seem to have reversed over the years.

In 2006, 64.5% of pastors thought that attendance was the greatest challenge. Many pastor friends tell me they are embarrassed that nobody comes out for special services. However, even today I've seen pastors who successfully promote special events with great attendance every night and have an enthusiastic attitude that's contagious. Leadership, fasting, prayer and promotion remain the keys to successful meetings. The second challenge in the 2006 survey involved finances according to 20.1% of pastors, and then lastly, securing the evangelist with 5.9% of the responses.

You must remember, a pastor knows their community and how their congregation will respond, so I am never offended at their choice of services. They may want to have a Sunday only; Friday through Sunday; Saturday through Monday; Sunday through Wednesday, or some other series of services. They know what might work best, and if they ask you what you think, be ready to share some options that might work for them.

I have some pastors who like the Saturday, Sunday, Monday venue because there is no conflict with Friday night football and the services only include one workday. You just need to have different options that you can give to church leaders. But remember, attendance continues to be one of the major challenges today and seems to have played a part in why many churches no longer have Sunday evening and midweek services.

Since special meeting attendance is decreasing, the offerings also potentially decrease so that you don't necessarily have enough revenue coming in to meet the financial needs. Several different strategies can help generate enough revenue for special services. Two of these that I mentioned in Chapter three surrounded the use of faith promises or a designated fund with special offerings.

But honestly, it's all about priorities. What's the priority of the pastor as the leader within that church? Some extreme situations arise when attendance begins to decline so badly that a pastor lacks enough money to provide for himself or herself. That's why we must have suggestions to help pastors raise funds for special services if opportunities arise in our conversations.

We must think of ingenious ways for smaller churches to afford hosting evangelists. Those are the ones that really need the ministry of the evangelist. A larger church might have an evangelist's quarters or help with accommodations so a smaller church can gain some spiritual infusion through special services or events. Sometimes you can work to minister in a sectional round robin, and you might speak at 2 or 3 churches in a section. These are just some of the options that we, as evangelists, can work on to keep from being a burden to pastors financially. Remember, our goal is to be a blessing and a gift.

Question seven discussed the negative characteristics of evangelists. Sadly, what really impacted pastors negatively in 1996 was an evangelist who was financially demanding according to 40.3% of pastors. Apparently, there was a lot of manipulation at the altar as 36.3% of pastors stated, while 33.1% had a non-servant attitude. Unfortunately, those were still in the top three on the 2006 survey, with the first two reversed. How sad that altar manipulation rose to number one according to 44.8% of pastors, followed by financially demanding and the non-servant attitude.

Some evangelists prefer to take their own offerings, and I have heard of a few guest speakers who have taken multiple offerings during one service for ministry projects. Personally, I feel that is way out of line and an affront to the Gospel. I have always found the pastor capable of more influence on an offering than I could ever have and his or her appeal should be sufficient for you. If you have special needs, you should talk with the pastor about these and ask if he or she has any suggestions to help you in that area.

In some cases, the guest speaker does not even tell the pastor about their intentions in this regard. That really goes behind the pastor's back and sheds a negative light upon all potential guests. I don't know how people get away with that. If I was a pastor that would not be something I would allow and I would talk with my guest prior to a service about the offering. If they began to do something we had not agreed upon, I would not hesitate to walk to the podium and thank our brother or sister for their time and ask them to be seated.

Lastly, our surveys asked how evangelists could be more effective? In 1996, a relevant message ranked as number one with 74.6% pastors saying so, dynamic altar services or a witness of valid ministry earned second place with 72.9%, and better correspondence ranked third with 21.8% of pastors saying so. The 2006 survey revealed that over that ten-year span, pastors felt that evangelists could be most effective by evidence of an anointed ministry according to 27.6% of pastors.

Secondly, pastors felt that evangelists should have a relevant message—not just a good message. Time and time again, pastors shared how an evangelist would come in and preach a canned sermon that wasn't really relevant to them and didn't really touch their people. They could tell that the evangelist had not prayed and heard from God for a fresh message to give to those people.

As an evangelist, there are times when God tells you to preach a message that you've preached before. One pastor said, "It's ok to preach left-overs but you ought to serve them hot." What he inferred was that you needed to hear from the Holy Spirit—or "hear from Heaven" as is often said—that a particular message was what you needed to share. If you're hearing from Heaven, then the Lord will anoint the message that he's given you to preach. However, as an evangelist you should always be working on a fresh message—work hard to stay fresh.

Relevance also means that you understand and relate well to your audience. Pastors want you to be relevant to the people in their congregations, as well as to the issues they may be facing. You should be aware of whether a church reflects a more seeker sensitive setting or an old-time, Pentecostal, Spirit-filled, camp meeting style setting. The type of people present will determine how you present the Gospel message. In a seeker setting, you won't use a lot of churchy language that people don't understand. If you're in an old-time camp meeting, then it's okay to talk about being washed in the blood, pew-sitters and a lot of other terminologies that young, non-Christians don't know anything about.

Additionally, the survey revealed that every evangelist should strive to keep a servant attitude as mentioned earlier in this chapter. Sadly, as shown by both surveys, this aspect of effective evangelistic ministry cannot be stressed enough. Maintaining a servant attitude, with humility and sensitivity to the Holy Spirit are really going to go a long way in strengthening any pastor and evangelist relationship. Additionally, the communication that you have with pastors and your continued dialog with them will only build greater levels of trust and possibly open more doors of ministry. Be a friend and help them achieve God's vision for that church in their community.

Regardless of your gifts, every evangelist can work at being a better servant. You can be an assertive servant—I hope you are! I don't have to apologize for what I do if I am following the Lord Jesus Christ and preaching the Word of God. Are there other people that can preach better than me? You bet. Are there people that operate in the gifts better than I do? Sure. But you know what? I'm working to be a servant of the most high God who loves me and cares about me. So, I don't have to apologize to anybody for the ministry I do as long as I'm following Christ. I'm not preaching to impress anybody but my Heavenly Father. And if I'm preaching the Word of God and the Word that He's told me to preach, then I don't have to apologize to the pastor or to anybody who might get offended.

You never know who God might want to speak to through you. So, you must come to that place where you don't need to gain the acceptance or approval of people. And the Lord has to bring us all as Holy Spirit empowered ministers and leaders to a place where we don't have an inferiority complex about who we are or what we're doing. God has called pastors and evangelists to work together and do what we do.

If we're hearing from Heaven and saying what God wants us to say, then we don't have to apologize to anybody. We can be assertive in our servant attitude. You never heard Jesus going around saying: "You know I don't preach very good and you probably don't want me to come to your church, but if you feel sorry for me then give me a chance."

No, he was a servant following the will of His Heavenly Father. He washed other people's feet, but when it came to the Word of God, he was bold; and it was that boldness of the Holy Spirit of God that rose up in Him. He preached with authority, and that same authority has been given to each of us who preach the Gospel. If we'll focus on Christ and give Him all the glory, He'll give us some great relationships with church leaders that will advance the Kingdom of God.

Survey Comparisons 1996—2006

Survey of Leading Pastors about Evangelists – 1996
(From Davis, James O.,
The Pastor's Best Friend, Gospel Publishing House, 1997, p. 132)

Pastors' Survey of Evangelists November 2006
(Online electronic survey conducted by the AG National Evangelists Office, Oct-Nov, 2006)

1. Main qualities looked for in evangelists:
   a. Integrity (80.6%)
   b. Solid Bible preacher (70.1%)
   c. Fruitful ministry (60.2%)

1. Main qualities looked for in evangelists:
   a. Integrity (86%)
   b. Solid Bible Preacher (85.1%)
   c. **Servant-hood / humility** (73.8%)

2. Hosted a campaign within the last year?
   a. Yes (80.6%)
   b. No (19.4%)

2. Hosted a campaign within the last year?
   = Not asked

3. Was your last campaign successful?
   a. Yes (85.2%)
   b. No (14.8%)

3. Hosted a successful evangelistic / revival campaign in the last 2-3 years?
   a. Yes (65.3%)
   b. No (34.7%)

4. Why was your campaign successful?
   a. Souls saved (60.7%)
   b. Holy Spirit baptisms (48.5%)
   c. Dynamic preaching (47.7%)

4. Why was your campaign successful?
   a. Souls saved (47.6%)
   b. Personal needs met (46.4%)
   c. Holy Spirit Baptisms (44.8%)

5. How often do you invite evangelists?
   a. 1-3 times per year (87.9%)
   b. 4+ times per year (6.3%)
   c. Never (5.8%)

5. How often do you invite evangelists?
   a. Usually 1 time per year (37.1%)
   b. 2 or more times a year (31.9%)
   c. Less than once a year (24.1%)

6. Greatest challenge about evangelists:
   a. Right evangelist (54.7%)
   b. Attendance (37.0%)
   c. Finances (8.3%)

6. Greatest challenge of long meetings?
   a. Attendance (64.5%)
   b. Finances (20.1%)
   c. Securing the evangelist (5.9%)

7. Negative characteristics of evangelists:
   a. Financially demanding (40.3%)
   b. Altar manipulation (36.3%)
   c. Non-servant (33.1%)

7. Negative characteristics of evangelists:
   a. Altar manipulation (44.8%)
   b. Financially demanding (44.6%)
   c. Non-servant attitude (36%)

8. How can evangelists be more effective?
   a. Relevant Message (74.6%)
   b. Dynamic altar services (72.9%)
   c. Better correspondence (21.8%)

8. How can evangelists be more effective?
   a. Evidence of anointed ministry (27.6%)
   b. Relevant Message (24.9%)
   c. Servant Attitude (23%)

CHAPTER 5

Scheduling & Ministry Insights

It has been said that scheduling and finances are the two most dreaded things with which an evangelist contends. You battle finances, especially in the early years of your ministry, and you will almost always have to work on your schedule to some degree. One thing you must always remember; this is the Lord's ministry so don't take negative responses personally. You will find that people are still people and sometimes we all have bad days. Determine to always "take the high road" in your responses and attitude. I have actually had phone conversations turn around and meetings scheduled even though it was not a very pleasant conversation initially.

CONNECTING

Although there are some organizations that support their evangelists and itinerant ministers, exponentially more denominations allow these ministries to function within the arena of a "faith-based" organization. This means that whatever offerings and support come in on a weekly or monthly basis for the itinerant minister are the sole financial provisions available to that ministry. In these situations, it is paramount for the itinerant minister to maintain a fairly full schedule of meetings while making provision for special Sundays and holidays when services will be hard to schedule due to other activities of the church.

Determine the audience or prospective people and organizations you are trying to reach, i.e. churches, schools, etc. Then determine the distance you can travel on any given weekend. If you feel that you can manage traveling 5 hours for a morning service (roughly from Springfield, Missouri to Memphis, Tennessee), then take a map of the USA and, with a pencil and string, draw a circle around your potential travel area. Within your circle, you should make divisions or sections of some kind to help you organize your mailings and phone call follow-ups. Make a list, by whatever means you have available, of the individuals, churches, and institutions you would like to eventually send information to, along with their phone numbers.

There are several different approaches that are utilized in trying to connect with pastors and gain potential meetings. The most important thing you can do prior to making any contact is to pray that God would help guide your calls, commitments, and attitude. Whether you start by writing letters or calling on the phone, attitude is crucial, and the help of the Holy Spirit is paramount.

Of the many methods utilized in connecting with pastors and organizational leaders for special meetings, we will touch on some of the following: Prayer; mailing material; calling; mailing promo packets first, then follow-up calling followed by mailing additional materials as requested; as well as calling contacts first and then mailing ministry information packets.

PRAYER

God has moved upon some itinerant ministers to pray for their ministry opportunities and not to call anyone! This is indeed a special calling and not one that everyone will be able to embrace. However, I have witnessed some individuals who have become braggadocios about this aspect of their ministry—which can be a warning sign of things to come. But God does indeed open doors that we often would not consider, and "will even make a way in the wilderness" (Isaiah 43:19 KJV)! As God opens doors for you, many times the pastor of a welcoming church will make calls to other pastor friends on your behalf. The caution is that you should not expect this or manipulate others just so you can say you have "never" had to make a phone call to anyone.

MAILING

Some evangelists like using a system that involves only mailing out materials to prospective people with no follow-up communication. The objective is to mail a certain quantity out every week in hopes that pastors will read the materials and be enticed to call. With the expense of all those materials and the fact that pastors receive "lots" of mailings (most of which go into "file 13"—also known as the trash can), this could really be a waste of time and money.

CALLING

Some evangelists who have been on the field of ministry for a while use the "call only" method of connecting with pastors. Most individuals who utilize this approach have received a referral to call certain church leaders, or they already had a relationship with the pastor being called.

....

Take Note: *Using the phone for communication has its own set of etiquette that evangelists must consider. Since it is relatively easy to discern whether someone is excited or depressed over the phone, you should have an attitude of excitement and confidence about what God is doing in your ministry when calling for meetings. Who wants to invite someone who is depressed about their own ministry?! Share with excitement what God is doing in your life and ministry—focus on the positive, not the negative, but be honest in your communications. Determine from the start of your ministry that you will endeavor to be a minister who lives a life of integrity and honesty. A good reputation, in and of itself, will take you farther in life than a boat full of charisma and false statements about salvations and miracles in your ministry.*

....

MAIL, CALL, MAIL

The "mail, call, mail" system utilizes a weekly mailing of letters, followed by a phone call ten days to two weeks later (just enough time for individuals to receive the mail and read it—hopefully). Then mail any additional information requested. The problem with this was somewhat stated above; the fact that postage and material expenses become hindrances, and pastors receive so much mail that most solicitations go into the trash can. Albeit, if a pastor friend is writing a letter of introduction for you, then a follow-up call shortly after the letter is sent is obviously necessary.

If you use the "mail, call, mail" (or even the "mail alone") approach make sure you keep your mailings organized. To help facilitate a somewhat systematic approach you may want to send out approximately 25 to 50 letters per week. You might want to lean towards the 25 (or less) depending on your workload. Two weeks after the initial mailing, follow-up with a phone call (remember, some pastors are bi-vocational so you will only get them on Saturdays—maybe). This will allow the letters to arrive at their destination and give everyone at least a week to read them. When you call, the conversation will vary a bit depending on each individual's response, but initially, the conversation could go something like this (please be yourself and write out what you are going to say if you don't really know—there will always be some variations):

"Hi, my name is _____ and I was just checking on the letter I sent out a couple of weeks ago. I apologize if I called at a bad time." [Pause for any response] "I didn't know whether you had been able to look over the information I sent a couple of weeks ago or not. I know pastors' schedules are pretty hectic, but God seems to be growing our ministry, and I am currently working on our schedule for next [spring, etc...] and did not know whether there might be any possibilities up in your area?"

Take Note: *Always err on the side of caution by using appropriate titles of respect and position, as well as saying "ma'am" or "sir," etc...*

You have now quickly laid all your intentions right up front, and the ball is in the pastor's court. The conversation will vary from this point on, and you can share more specifics if asked. If the pastor says "I'm already booked up this year" (often their way to say no), you should still ask something like: "Would you like for me to give you a call back later this year, or do you feel that this might not work for your church at this time?" With this type of statement, you are giving the pastor an "out," and they will appreciate this far more than if you try to nail them to a specific obligation. Everyone likes options. Follow-up materials can be sent as requested.

Take Note: *Maintain a professional attitude whenever you are corresponding with others. Don't be pushy or manipulative, which sometimes obtains a short-term booking. The pastor will say yes to appease you and then cancel a month later. This is sometimes referred to as "button-holing" a pastor— forcing them into a situation that they don't appreciate. Allow the Holy Spirit to open doors for you! On this same note—don't beg for services! The Lord has not called us to be beggars (Psalm 37:25). If it seems like every door is closed, it is time to go into your prayer closet for a time of fasting and prayer in order to discern the will of God in that situation.*

CALL, MAIL

The "call, mail" system seems to be the most efficient and frugal way to connect with pastors and leaders. Although "cold" phone calls (no referral) can work, having a referral from another pastor, known by the pastor being called, is best. Don't ask other evangelists for referrals (unless they are dear friends) since most evangelists are very protective of their relationships and pastors would usually rather have the recommendation of a pastor they know than an evangelist. Albeit, just because another pastor may give you a name or list of names to call does not mean you are guaranteed instant access—the pastor you are calling, and the Holy Spirit, have the last word. Once you have made contact, you can send additional information if desired, and definitely send a confirmation letter if a service date is agreed upon.

Since a majority of pastors shepherd smaller congregations, you will find that quite a few pastors are bi-vocational. That said, you may not be able to catch them via phone during the day, but you may have to call the church number towards evening or on the weekends. DO NOT call a pastor's home or cell number unless that pastor has specifically given you permission to call their home or cell phone numbers.

Some other methods, which seem to irritate more than provide opportunities, involve electronic mailing lists that somehow find their way into your email account. Whether it is "spam" email or a "listserv" that you just happened to find out you are on (even though you never subscribed), some individuals feel that broadcasting their availability will be viewed as legitimacy for their ministry. This actually works against them and should not be encouraged.

....

Take note: *if you do have an email database that you utilize to send out ministry newsletters and updates, please ensure that you are getting permission from pastors to promote the signup sheet, and make sure that you are not adding names without permission.*

....

When calling, you want to make sure that your presentation is only about 20-30 seconds. You may want to say something like this (also see the previous section):

Hi, my name is _____ and I was wondering if pastor _____ was in this morning? Hi pastor _____, did

I call at a bad time? If so I can call you at another time that's more convenient. [Wait for response—even if long] [If o.k.] My name is _____ and I'm an evangelist here in [City, State]. We were with pastor _____ this past week and he encouraged me to give you a call. We were looking for possible ministry opportunities in your area this coming [spring, fall, etc...] and did not know whether there might be any opportunities with you?

Note: Some pastors like to intimidate people who call by remaining silent. If they do not respond the first time, feel free to ask again: "Is this a bad time, Pastor _____?" Then just wait for their response, they usually say something sooner or later. If they answer yes, ask "Is there a time when I might be able to call back that would be better for you?" Some people are just negative and if you feel that things are digressing just say something like: "I'm sorry to have bothered you today. I pray you have a good day." (This is a bit unsettling the first time it happens to you.) If they answer no, you can continue on.

You will most likely find that Mondays and Fridays are not very good days to call anyone, but follow God's leading and ask the secretary, if available when a good time might be to try and connect with the pastor if they are not in when you call. One thing you must do when calling is to keep a phone log of some kind. It can be homemade and simple, but should contain: the church or organization called, phone number (makes for a great quick reference when calling back), pastor/leader's name, date called, and comments—like when they would like you to call back or that you just got their voice mail. Good Luck!

INFORMATIONAL MATERIALS

Your mailing materials should look neat and professional—even if you are utilizing email and the Internet to provide materials to your host organization. I always tell young evangelists to start where they are—not where someone else is. They don't need all the fancy, full color, posters and brochures like some evangelists who have been in ministry for years. When I first started, I bought an okay computer and the nicest printer I could afford. I printed my own posters and glued our prayer cards on them.

We decided to spend our money on our prayer cards and printer since we would be creating our own newsletters to send out. As you grow, you always strive to keep your materials fresh—don't keep using a photo that's twenty years old! Be innovative and use your creative talents and the Holy Spirit's leading to make a lasting impression.

Email is a great (and currently cheap) medium of correspondence. More and more pastors today want to correspond via email. If you have a website, direct pastors desiring more information to your site, but make sure you take the time (or someone else does) to keep your website fresh and up to date with relevant content and pastor-friendly resources. Some websites are even free, but make sure they look professional before you start directing anyone to them. If you are going to incorporate a blog, make sure you have the time to maintain it!

Continue to seek ways to improve your materials as opportunity allows. Work on new designs or a new look every couple of years if possible. Your promotional materials represent you and people do "judge a book by its cover" even though we are not supposed to do that. A word of caution: please, please, please be honest in your promotional materials. I can't tell you how many websites I have viewed in which the evangelist was "the most sought after" evangelist. How could all of them be "the most sought after?"

REFERRALS AND ENDORSEMENTS

During scheduled meetings, you are always looking for additional meetings and folks who might give you referrals or endorsements. After an exceptionally good service, you may feel led to ask the pastor, where you are ministering, whether he or she knows of anyone who might be blessed by your ministry. You can easily facilitate this by saying that you are always looking for opportunities to expand the ministry's effectiveness and wondered whether he or she knew of anyone you might be able to call for ministry.

When seeking referrals or endorsements, it is imperative to wait for the right timing and guidance from the Holy Spirit. Nobody enjoys feeling used, and that is the last impression you want to leave with someone. So usually you would wait until after a good meeting or series of meetings before inquiring. Some pastors will actually volunteer to call others for you*, or may be open to writing a letter of recommendation*. You may also feel free, especially with a closer relationship, to ask whether they "would be open to sharing an endorsement, or a sentence or two about the ministry that I could include in future communication with others?"*

....

*Take Note: *These last three points are sensitive areas—do not try to manipulate pastors into helping you. Allow the Holy Spirit to work and confirm your ministry. Only approach this avenue if the pastor brings up the subject, or you know the pastor extremely well.*

....

Whatever method(s) of connecting with church leaders that God leads you to use, you must immerse it in prayer and strive to be a great ambassador for the Lord Jesus Christ.

CONFIRMING

After God has graciously opened up a door of ministry to you and a meeting date has been scheduled, a confirmation letter should be sent that same week—or day if possible. We live in an action-packed world, and the ministry is no exception. Pastors have so many different hats they wear, and it is easy for schedules and appointments to unintentionally get lost in the shuffle of life. So many people and events are pulling for a pastor's attention, and if not careful, a double booking can even occur.

In your confirmation letter (see example in Appendix A) you should open with a small paragraph of personal greeting and any relevant personal news that might be going on with yourself. The second paragraph should thank the pastor or organization "for the opportunity to minister on (insert date of ministry here)." You always include the ministry dates that were agreed upon to help minimize any confusion. If the wrong date was inadvertently given, then seeing it (putting the date in bold print may also be helpful) in the letter will allow the individual scheduling the opportunity to quickly call and reschedule the correct date with you.

In your closing paragraph ensure that you thank the pastor or organization again, and note that you will be calling them a few weeks prior to the ministry date to check in and get any service details. If you have scheduled the meeting one to two years ahead (or more), you need to ensure you are contacting them at least a year out, and especially 6 months ahead of time to ensure you are still on the calendar. Postcards, as well as email if permissible, can be cost effective here.

CONTACTING

At least one month ahead of the scheduled meeting you should be sending out any promotional materials, posters, ad slicks (camera ready), invitation card samples, etc., for the host church. If you are scheduled in a larger venue at district or national events, you may need to provide promotional materials much sooner. Always check with the organization or church to accommodate their desires.

Many itinerant ministers today have a majority of their promotional materials on their websites. Some evangelists have a secure area of their website that pastors or organizational leaders can go to for materials. The evangelist gives a password to the hosting church for access to these areas, which saves material and postage costs for the guest.

Always call two to four weeks out to find out necessary details of an upcoming service and helpful considerations you should know. Some items you should check on include:

Hotel / accommodations: As a guest, you should always try to be sensitive to a church's financial abilities. Some churches always provide hotel rooms, while others have evangelist quarters (a room in the local church building specifically built and dedicated to itinerant ministers or missionaries), while others actually have a room in their own home to accommodate their guests.

Although staying in a pastor's home is an extremely nice gesture, and we have stayed in several, I would recommend trying to keep some privacy for you and your family during scheduled services. If you must stay in the pastor's home, those with a basement-type apartment have been a wonderful experience for us. I talk more about this in Chapter 6.

I do not mean to be unkind when I share my preferences; I just know that the standards by which we function as a family are not necessarily the same standards someone else will use. I also know that I am extremely social (as most evangelists are), and if I'm around people, I will want to visit with them. It is an added benefit to you and the church where you have been invited, for you to have a place of solitude away from everyone so that you can touch the throne room of Heaven and hear what God wants to say to that particular congregation instead of letting your time slip away due to socializing or "fellowshipping."

We have never made a point of demanding a hotel room, but have tried to be gracious in suggesting it. If a pastor does not mention hotel accommodations during our conversation, I might ask them if they know of a good hotel in the area that we could stay at. Oftentimes this will help remind the pastor, who has a million other things on his or her mind, about accommodations. They usually offer to take care of the accommodations, but if not, they usually recommend a few places. If they don't offer to help us with accommodations, we seek the Lord's guidance and realize this may be a time of sowing seed into that ministry.

If asked what we prefer, we also say that we don't want to be a burden to the church but that a hotel would be a huge blessing for us. On some occasions, we have even offered to take care of the cost if needed.

I have said all that to say, you will undoubtedly stay in a plethora of accommodations, and likely have many stories to tell through the years. We have even stayed in a 5th wheel RV on more than one occasion that someone in the church had. In all things strive to be gracious and appreciative of what the church can provide—it may be a true sacrifice on their part to even have a guest speaker. And as usual, God always makes up the difference down the road at another service somewhere.

....

Take Note: *If you have been blessed with accommodations at a local hotel or motel, try to get a copy of the closing receipt if at all possible. Some hotels are set up to give copies to guests in direct-billed situations, and others are extremely hesitant to provide copies. The copy is purely a safeguard for you concerning what will be charged to the church. I heard a true story about an evangelist who came to a church, and when the church finally got the bill for his hotel stay, there were charges for adult pornographic movies on his room bill. Needless to say, the pastor was not happy about this and called the evangelist. The evangelist swore that he had never watched anything like that while at the hotel. Upon further questioning of the hotel personnel and noting the time of the charges, it was discovered that the cleaning personnel had decided to watch some pornographic movies while cleaning up the room! As an itinerant minister, your reputation is everything, so guard it carefully.*

....

When traveling by vehicle with a family, it is a good idea to take some cots and covers or sleeping bags to make the most of unpleasant situations. If you have two children and are in a room with two double beds (or one king size bed), it may be better to set up cots for the children so that you and your spouse get a good night's sleep.

If you are leaving right after all day services, inquire about whether there is a place to rest between services. You may want your children to rest in the afternoon (and you may want to as well) since it may possibly be a late night getting back home or to your next destination. Sometimes the only place to stay is in a room in the church, and the cots come in real handy then! Whatever you do, don't invite yourself to the pastor's home.

Dress code: It is always a good idea to ask the pastor what is the normal dress code for Sunday morning, Sunday night, and weeknight services. The last thing you want to do as a guest speaker is to be offensive in your attire. Although we are not supposed to "judge a book by its cover," that is exactly what most people do as we mentioned earlier. You don't necessarily want to wear the latest and most expensive fashion (suit or dress) in a small country church where most folks are struggling to even pay their bills.

Neither do you want to wear your nice suit and tie at youth camp services! As public speakers in the spotlight and as representatives of Jesus Christ, we strive to appear professional. However, sometimes we need to ask ourselves; who is our audience and what will help us "connect" with those to whom we are sent to minister?

Bible translation used: This may seem a bit mundane, but it's important. Realizing that there are differing opinions surrounding the translations of Scripture today begs us to mention this. The whole point of this section is to help us realize we need to do what is necessary to "connect" with our audience. Let me illustrate with a simple point. No one today preaches in "*Koine*" (pronounced 'coy-nay') Greek, and no one talks in the "King's English" of the 1600s. In many respects, the early English letters look different and words that meant one thing in the 1600s mean an embarrassing translation today if the same wording was used. So too, many "non-Christians" will probably not understand the King James Version language of the Scriptures.

But many other areas of the country are immersed in tradition and Christian heritage, and using anything other than the King James Version of the Scriptures would label you as a heretic. If you are a true studier of the Word of God, you utilize many study helps that take you back to the original biblical languages of Hebrew, Aramaic, and Greek. Use the language today that is understood and respected by those to whom you minister.

Ask the pastor what he or she uses so that you can be a glove on his or her hand and your Scripture translation won't hinder someone from coming into God's Kingdom. Using the "common" translation will also help you connect with the local congregation easier since that translation will be what they are used to hearing.

Length of sermons: If you have been in ministry any length of time you have probably heard about the evangelist that preached for an hour and a half in the morning service! The people were so scared of a repeat that no one showed up for the evening service. As a guest, you should try to follow the pastor's normative sermon time. If the Holy Spirit begins to move, everyone will most likely stay with you and not complain. But just to preach that long because you feel you have something to say is a great way never to get invited back.

Another thing to remember is that most churches are a little more time sensitive in the morning service than at other times. Since you are most likely trying to introduce your ministry and connect with the people in the morning service, you should strive to keep messages a little shorter so that you have time for God to do something during the altar time. If you preach up until the last minute of a normal service, most people are heading for the door. The main point is to be sensitive to the working-class person you are trying to minister to and realize—with evening services—that they have to get up the next day and go to work. The Spirit will ultimately guide you if you let Him.

Directions: The last thing you want to do is show up late to your service! Make sure you ask for directions to the hotel and church. Make sure you write down church times and ask the pastor if there is a time he would prefer you arrive. If you have family, you should really strive to arrive so that they can be a part of the Sunday School time if the church has one. Oftentimes guest speakers want to find a solitary place away from everyone to go over their message and make sure they are spiritually and mentally prepared for the upcoming service. Some churches have multiple services so arrive early and be prepared to help the pastor with anything needed. If you are unfamiliar with the area, utilize state and city maps, or print off copies of Internet directions.

Transportation: In your follow-up conversation, you will need to let the pastor know whether you are driving and whether you will have an RV or not. This discussion may already come up during your initial booking as well. If you have an RV you need to see what type of water, sewer, and electrical hook-ups the church may have. Some churches have hook ups at the church, while others will have to help you in other ways. There may be an RV Park close by, but if not, you will have to "dry camp" with your camper for a day or so. At the very least, you need to find out where a dump station is located—sometimes, large truck stops have these facilities.

If you are flying there are several things to consider. First, you need to let the pastor know up front that you will probably be flying in on a Saturday, or whatever day is conducive to the meeting, and ensure that this mode of travel is acceptable with the pastor. If you are flying, notification of that expense should be sent as soon as a reservation is made, and some travel agencies will even do this for you—for a small fee.

Again, you should not necessarily be demanding, but sending a note to let them know that you have just purchased your airfare for the trip and share the total amount of the ticket. Then you might want to share "if there is any way you could help with any portion of this expense we would greatly appreciate it."

Also, you may want to inquire about whether someone might pick you up or whether you will be getting a rental vehicle. Even if you are driving, a note of appreciation and sharing the mileage and financial expense to you should be considered. Many in leadership just do not think about the cost of travel unless you are flying. This is not generally done on purpose, it is just not thought of, and a gentle note can be a great way to convey the need present. One evangelist asks churches to pray with them that the Lord would meet specific travel expenses in their letters.

Time you plan on arriving: You should ensure that you let the pastor know your expected time of arrival. Many times, the pastor uses the fellowship time over dinner on Saturday night to get to know you and your ministry better. Do not secretly plan on showing up every time just prior to dinner so that you can get a free meal! Plan on coming a little later if possible so that the pastor can bring up the option of having dinner with him and his family, and you won't be seen as someone always trying to take advantage of other people.

CONDUCTING

When it comes time to actually arrive at your destination and hold your meeting or series of meetings there are a few things you should keep in mind:

Be a blessing to the pastor. The sole purpose of your visit is to obey God for that moment and those people who will receive your ministry. But you must remember that you are there to help the pastor in any way possible—within reason. You may be called upon to help with nursing home services, hospital visits, teaching Sunday School, or some other activity that the pastor feels would be helpful. This is also often a part of your time when the pastor can talk with you about issues being faced in that area.

They are on the front lines of ministry and usually, have no one that they can talk to or confide in—so you become a sounding board. As I have mentioned before, your conversations are confidential, and you should never gain the reputation as one who has loose lips—or prone to talk about things other people have confided in you.

Always direct positive comments back to the pastor. When people convey their appreciation for your ministry or any other number of absolutely marvelous things they could say about your ministry, redirect their praise back towards the pastor. You just might say: "You should make sure and thank your pastor for having the foresight of scheduling special services like this." Or "your pastor is the only reason I/we are able to be here—make sure you let him (or her) know how much these services have meant to you."

Pastors remain behind when you leave, and anything you can do to help elevate their ministry in the eyes of parishioners not only helps the pastor but also strengthens your relationship with them. They can begin to trust your ministry and have confidence that you are not there to steal their church or their people.

Never partner with problem people. Sometime in your travels, you will assuredly come across individuals who play the devil's advocate. They are always complaining about something and will want to draw an unsuspecting visitor into their way of thinking if they feel you might be won to their side. You must never side with these types of folks. Encourage them to share their feelings with the pastor, and you need to confide derogatory comments and people to the pastor at the earliest convenience. You are there for the pastor, and you should remember that you are a guest in someone else's home so-to-speak. Act as you would want someone to act in your home.

Never be deceptive about mailing lists. Mailing lists are an important part of itinerant ministry in that they allow us to share insights, needs, and testimonies with those who are interested. Some may want to support you in prayer, while others may want to contribute financially to your ministry. Some may just want to be informed. It is one thing to mail or email a copy of your newsletter to the church where you have ministered, but it is another to solicit people to sign up without the pastor's permission. This does not mean to ask permission in front of everyone while you are behind the pulpit. Who would appreciate that kind of pressure? Always gain permission for mailing lists and anything else if possible, prior to the initial service.

Be professional. You are a representative of Jesus Christ and a leader within the church at large. You must conduct yourself in a manner which honors God and hold yourself to a higher standard of holiness and dedication to God than others who have not been called to vocational ministry. Ministers who are slothful, stingy, ill-mannered, flirtatious, have a bad attitude, or any other number of denigrating characteristics will undermine God's ministry and will create a dichotomy which is unscriptural, as well as just plain unchristian.

Ensure safeguards are in place. Safeguards and accountability measures must be a normal part of your ministry. Take another accountability partner with you if you do not minister with family. If no accountability partners are feasible, set safeguards for yourself. Some safeguards to think about may be: Never be left alone with the opposite sex; leave the television off if you struggle with temptations; install special software on your computer if inappropriate surfing is an issue in your life; call your spouse regularly to check in; and any other ways you can think of to help keep you in check.

....

Take Note: *It is easy to say: "I don't have issues like that and only people not right with God have to deal with that kind of stuff." But as soon as you adopt that mentality, the enemy already has the advantage of self-righteousness or pride in your life. We are all fallen creatures, and without God's help, we would all fail miserably. Stay in the Scriptures and stay accountable.*

....

Don't manipulate people with money. Because itinerant ministry can often be a time of "feast or famine," especially nice offerings, have a tendency of challenging our spirituality. When the bills are stacking up, and the kids are sick, and your only mode of transportation is on its last legs, it is difficult "not" to start thinking of how you are going to get through those kinds of challenges. But God alone will supply all our needs, "according to His riches in glory by Christ Jesus" (Phil 4:19, KJV). By immersing ourselves in Scripture and devoting ourselves to prayer, we can avoid the temptation of manipulating others for financial gain.

Product tables should NOT be your priority. As I mentioned in Chapter 4, you should communicate with the pastor concerning product tables and resources that you may want to share. I occasionally hear of instances where evangelists focus more on their product tables than the altar. As an evangelist, you may often subsidize your ministry with a product table. The product table itself is not bad and often helps pay for fuel, travel expenses, and the lean times during the year when services are few and far between. But you have been called of God to minister to those individuals who have come to hear a word from God.

If you have a product table, it is always preferable to have the pastor mention your product table for you if he or she so desires. If they prefer that you present your materials, you should make these presentations as brief as possible—about three minutes maximum. At the conclusion of the service, don't leave the altar to conduct business at your product table! If needed, have a partner help you with your table or request assistance from the church.

Some churches are happy to assist with this, but you need to check to see what the pastor desires. Be willing to provide a moneybag with a set amount of change for anyone helping with your table. Some evangelists utilize the honor system successfully, as well as offering products for a recommended donation. Make sure you check on each state's tax laws prior to setting up your product table to ensure you are in compliance with government regulations.

COMMITTING

A crucial part of any ministry is a commitment to excellence. If anything is worth doing it is worth doing right. Whether you are creating a newsletter, website, prayer card or developing some other aspect of ministry, it should be done with excellence in mind. Whatever you do, or create, it is a reflection of you. As a servant of Jesus Christ, we need to be mindful that we represent the King of Kings and Lord of Lords in every aspect of our ministries. If we strive to be pleasing to God with a pure and humble heart, He will work on our behalf to help our ministries be relevant and refreshing.

Another valuable part of ministry is committing to safeguard what God has entrusted to you. We must instill safeguards into our ministries because we all need accountability. No one is above correction or accountability, and this will not only keep us in the will of God—it will keep us from failing miserably and blemishing the Kingdom of God. When ministers of the Gospel fall, they usually take a multitude of people with them—those who believed in them and what God was doing through them.

Finally, we need to commit to the ministry itself. It's tough, and we need a solid resolve that we will not give up. It often takes two to four years of hard work before many itinerant ministries are established enough to be self-supportive, and there will be many valleys during that time. Sadly, there are some leaders who do not know how to treat guests, and some will hurt you and treat you less than a Christian should. But as a Spirit-empowered minister of the Gospel, you must always take the "high road." Don't retaliate, as that is the Lord's responsibility and one that he can aptly take care of without our fleshly intervention.

....

Take note: *This is a great area where a spiritual journal can really be a blessing and encouragement to you. During down times, you can read back through your spiritual journal and see where God has answered prayers, provided miraculously, and opened doors you never dreamed possible. Reading back through your journal can really be therapeutic spiritually, emotionally, and mentally. The enemy of your soul wants you to forget what God has done, but even Paul told us in Philippians 4:8, "Finally, brethren, whatsoever things are true, whatsoever things are honest, whatsoever things are just, whatsoever things are pure, whatsoever things are lovely, whatsoever things are of good report; if there be any virtue, and if there be any praise, think on these things." Meditating on the great things that God has done for us is a wonderful way to refresh ourselves in mind, body and spirit.*

....

CONCLUDING

Let the pastor know you have appreciated the opportunity. One important item you should remember to take care of after any ministry meeting is to send a thank you note, card, or personally typed letter of appreciation. Please ensure that you actually sign your letter!

I heard a story from one pastor of a guest speaker who sent materials to his church but never showed up for the service. The guest speaker had a staff of people and had double-booked himself for services on that day. If that were not bad enough, the speaker then sent a thank you letter to the church, thanking them for their time of ministry with the church! He did not show up, but then still sent a letter of appreciation for services that he never conducted—and did not even sign the letter that was sent. This kind of behavior obviously leaves a bad impression and displays an attitude of arrogance, which is never appreciated.

Keep a ministry journal. This is different from a spiritual journal. Your ministry journal helps you note songs sung, messages preached, names of the pastor and his/her family—significant dates, birthdays, and anniversaries. It can also help you remember the date of the service(s), what happened in the service(s)—people saved, baptized in the Holy Spirit, deliverances, etc. You can also take note of certain individuals like the sound person, youth pastor, etc…, as well as how the service flowed and directions on how to get to the church.

The ministry journal is simply a way for you to familiarize yourself with key aspects of a church that may help you connect a little easier the next time you are there. It may also help your awareness of sensitive issues or people that you should avoid. It is important to note that your journal should not be a "black book" listing all the bad things about a church and its members, but an informational tool to help with insights for future reference.

Knowing how to get to a church and the pastor's name, as well as the names of their spouse and children, show that you care enough to write such things down to remember them. You also should know how long the pastor likes to preach, the version of Scriptures preferred, PA system challenges, or opportunities that may avail themselves to you in the future.

The journal can also be a way to help you as you pray about messages that the Lord wants to speak through you to that congregation. As mentioned elsewhere in this book, you should always be working on new messages and hopefully striving to craft at least one new message a week. But there are times when the Holy Spirit speaks to our hearts to share messages that have been preached before.

Although we should never become complacent in our sermon prep, there are times when God leads us to pull out an older message and dust it off, perhaps even re-write it, for that certain occasion. When that happens, it is good to know what you have preached there previously to help you discern the leading of the Holy Spirit.

CONTINUING

Build strong relationships. If you plan on being in itinerant ministry for any length of time, you will find that relationships are your keys to a strong, life-long ministry. Working on our relationships is a daily necessity and one that can bear wonderful fruit for you.

....

Take Note: *The caution for every itinerant minister is to approach relationships as a personal necessity and not a business necessity. What I mean by that is we should resist the mindset that always plans some angle of what a relationship can do for us prior to engaging and developing that relationship. That is deceptive behavior and one that is not pleasing to God. But as an itinerant minister with speaking engagements being your sole means of income, this can be a tempting trap for all of us if we are honest.*

....

That said, we all need friends and folks who can speak into our lives. People who will help mentor us, as well as people that we can mentor and sow seeds of life experiences into, helping guide them in their pursuit of ministry.

When fostering relationships, we need to call pastors and individuals we have built friendships with just to say hello. Don't have a hidden agenda—be different—be genuine! Some people have special software to help them remember to call their list of acquaintances at specified times, while others just have a short list of friends they like to call every few months. When keeping in touch, make sure you are not a pest, and ensure sincerity is at the heart of your phone call or email. Your friends may have needs that you can pray for or just encourage them during some trying time in their ministry—be a Barnabas!

Year-end appreciation letters. Yearend appreciation letters can be a great way to stay in touch as well as convey appreciation for the invitations extended over the past year. If you send out newsletters make sure you send one to churches where you have been, as well as your support base and friends who you have made and will possibly pray for you.

....

Take Note: *If you send out letters or newsletters, DO NOT beg for money. Nothing turns people off more than to hear someone go on and on about money issues. It is one thing to mention the needs of your ministry but keep those brief. Focus most of your letter or newsletter on the blessings you have received and the miracles that God has done through your ministry. Believe that God will burden the hearts of those able to help you financially.*

....

Contact follow-up. The great thing about having a phone log is that it allows you an opportunity to connect with church leaders that have told you to contact them later in the year. You should always note those individuals who have asked you to give them a call later in the year so that you can faithfully follow-up and continue to gently work on fostering a new relationship.

Seek God for greater intimacy. Ministry is something that can be built by the methods of man, but can only be sustained and have eternal significance when God is involved in every aspect of the equation. Seeking God for a greater intimacy will not only help you as a minister, but will allow you oftentimes to hear more clearly what God is trying to say to you. Sometimes life can get so "loud" that we have difficulty hearing the "still, small voice" of God. Taking time out for yourself can be one of the most important things you do to "continue" in the ministry.

Attending conferences and special organization events. Every minister should attend their organization's special functions if at all possible. In the fellowship I am a part of we have sectional, district and national events. This is a great opportunity to connect with old friends and make new ones. Anytime there are activities where church leaders are getting together, we should try to attend if possible.

I have heard some itinerant ministers say, "I hate the politics" at work in those types of settings, and there is no way they are going. Honestly, there are politics at work in every aspect of life—the Church is no different. However, we all have the capacity to decide whether we will take part in those activities. A lot of genuine folks attend those functions, and it is a shame that we have opted to bow out to our own detriment. These events are usually scheduled far in advance and don't involve missing services to attend. If you are savvy in your scheduling, you can be a part of these opportunities and schedule services in the area as well.

When you do attend these types of functions, refuse to be the evangelist who hands their card out to everyone whether they want one or not. As a matter of fact, leave your calendar at home or in your pocket if you have a digital version. Every evangelist and itinerant minister knows his or her schedule fairly well for the next three to six months anyway. You know when you have some openings if the question comes up—or you can just opt to offer and call the individual at a later date because "you didn't bring your calendar with you." That will definitely surprise them.

Work at building friendships and strengthening existing relationships when attending these types of events. Pastors expect evangelists to push for meetings, so surprise them by not even bringing it up. Let the pastor bring up the invitation to possibly come if they want. Your goal is to be yourself and let people know that you would rather build friendships and destroy their stigma of the evangelist, than push for meetings and confirm their suspicions.

As you mingle with church leaders in new environments (sometimes being invited to attend events with a pastor you are with in special services), conversations will invariably lead to one's occupation. They will know soon enough that you are an itinerant minister and the fact that you did not bring that subject up may help change their opinion of the typical itinerant minister. Just your presence there at these special functions will bring an awareness of not just your ministry, but also the ministry of the evangelist. The old adage "out of sight out of mind" is true and if we don't maintain visibility, we will be forgotten that much sooner.

Lastly, as ministers, we all need to embrace times of ministry ourselves. I always enjoy the messages I hear at these special functions and oftentimes God wants to speak to me through the anointed preaching and teaching of God's Word. Do yourself a favor and plan on attending as many organizational events as you possibly can. I have scheduled more than one meeting by just being present when I met an "old friend" who had just been thinking about having some special services—isn't that just like God.

CANCELLATIONS

I can't think of a single person, in any vocation, who likes cancellations. As an itinerant minister, cancellations can be devastating since that means there will possibly be no income that week. However, when cancellations do come, try to be gracious and understanding since most church leaders realize how this affects itinerant ministers.

Upon notification of the cancellation, see if the possibility exists for re-scheduling. This may not be possible if the church has financial problems or personnel issues have been the impetus for canceling your time of ministry. However, if possible, rescheduling on the spot is less easily forgotten about and helps calm the situation for everyone.

The evangelist is relieved that he or she was not the reason for the cancellation and the church leader is relieved that he or she was able to make the best of a bad situation and hopefully have a great time of ministry at a later date. This helps foster a relationship of trust and appreciation between both parties. If the pastor asks you to call at a later date due to the ongoing situation, make sure you note that in your phone log, computer, etc.

If the cancellation is short-dated (30 days or less), you may inquire as to whether any gift might possibly be sent to help with your living expenses. I have never personally found that this approach worked when initiated by me since most church leaders are not open to this. Those pastors who have traveled, or have a heart for those who do, are more open to this and usually initiate that conversation with you.

However, if you have incurred airfare expenses in preparation for that meeting, you should let the pastor know that and ask how these expenses could best be reimbursed. Some itinerant ministers today use contracts for their meetings when flying has become a normal part of their travels.

Prayerfully, consider how to approach this subject if expenses need to be reimbursed and ask the pastor whether he or she knows of anyone you might call since you are already in the area. When you let them make the phone call, it is a huge help. You can also call other pastors where you are already scheduled to be in order to aid in filling a cancellation if possible.

Check with the district or sectional presbyter on whether they might know of any opportunities or open pulpits where you might be able to fill a slot. And when all else fails, and you can't fill a cancellation, utilize this as a period of time for seeking a greater intimacy with God. It may be His way of getting your attention!

COURTESY

As a guest, you must ensure that you don't take advantage of a church's hospitality and sacrifice. This includes a host family that you may be staying with, as well as the church leaders that have opened the door for your ministry. God has opened this door and every blessing and gift extended to you or your family must be seen in that light—so be a good steward of God's gifts!

Most pastors are busy folks; so, don't be offended if a pastor designates someone else to take you out for a meal due to unexpected circumstances. This can be a great time to build relationships with future church leaders. And you can rest assured that the pastor will hear all about how your time with the associate or substitute went later on.

You should also work to be a positive person—even when others complain. One thing I have learned over the years is that complainers are never satisfied. If they are not complaining about others to you, then they are complaining about you to others! Refuse to get bogged down in negative conversation and local church politics. When you have concerns over conversations that you may have, make sure that you let the pastor know about them. Not only does this help the pastor, but it also forges some wonderful relationships built on trust and appreciation. That church leader knows that he or she can trust you not to try and steal their church.

Finally, use your manners! If you don't know the proper etiquette or manners when you are in certain situations—like dining with the President—go to the library and read up on it. The quickest way to shut the door of ministry is to be offensive or an embarrassment merely by your lack of manners. When you find yourself in a new situation, and you're not sure what to do, just watch your host or hostess and follow their example. You must always remember that you are an ambassador for Jesus Christ—the Son of the Most High God.

CHAPTER 6

Some Seeds To Savor

In the pages that follow, I wanted to share some insights on various circumstances that I have encountered over the years, as well as some topics that I have received questions about. This is by no means an exhaustive list, but I pray that it would help you gain some sensitivity in dealing with similar situations in the event you happen to find yourself in one. As evangelists, we never know the circumstances surrounding a particular place of ministry until we are there and have sought God's leading through our ministry there. However, regardless of the situation, we must always remember that we represent Christ as His ambassadors.

A LITTLE GRACE IN GIVING

One thing that has apparently turned off more individuals to itinerant ministers and destroyed relationships with pastors has been the approach to the offering and finances. You should always talk with the senior pastor on his or her preference when it comes to the offering and any financial needs. Many pastors prefer to take the offering since they know their people and can present ministry needs in a way that is more fruitful and pleasing to everyone involved.

If the pastor grants you the privilege of taking the offering for your ministry, then do so with a humble heart and pure motives. When an itinerant minister uses manipulative tactics and fraudulent tricks to extort money from those in attendance at their meetings, the coffers may be overflowing, but the long-term effects are far from positive. If any minister uses tactics that manipulate and cause parishioners to feel condemnation when giving, you have done several damaging things to the Kingdom of God.

First, you have allowed God's people to associate a false teaching that the feeling of condemnation is a normal part of tithing and giving offerings. A feeling that is not healthy, nor a part of God's plan. God does desire a "joyful giver." After all, who wants to come to a church that condones making people feel bad in order to take up large offerings? If you are a part of anything that causes people to leave a church, you won't be invited back! We are called to help build the church—not tear it down.

Second, you have misrepresented God by your conduct and have become an offense to the Kingdom of God. Your ministry may be prospering financially, but spiritually you are "withering on the vine." The scriptures are extremely clear in detailing how God feels toward those stealing from his people. Jesus never lied to or manipulated people for offerings, and yes, He was God in the flesh and could cause money to appear even in a fish's mouth (Matt. 17:27). But, we don't need to steal because God still provides miraculously in many instances for His servants. God said in 2 Chronicles 16:9, *"For the eyes of the LORD run to and fro throughout the whole earth, to shew himself strong in the behalf of them whose heart is perfect toward him."(KJV)* God longs to show himself strong in behalf of those whose heart is perfect towards Him, and I can tell you it is quite exhilarating—and humbling—when He does it in your life.

Third, you have shown that you do not trust God to meet your needs. If you cannot exemplify faith in God, how can you expect others to trust God to give sacrificially? It is one thing to share needs, but a far different thing to badger, beg, or share outright lies about ministry needs. Always check with the pastor before sharing anything and make your appeals extremely brief. Try to let people who are not able to give an opportunity to feel at ease. You might ask the people to believe with you that God would meet or exceed your needs during the services with them. When an individual gives out of the abundance of their heart, not only is God pleased, but also the giver is blessed.

A person gives, usually not because they have a lot to give, but because they believe in your ministry, your vision, your passion, and your purpose. They want to be a part of something bigger than they are. They want to have a part in bringing souls into the Kingdom of God, letting the lame have an opportunity to walk again, the blind to see, the deaf to hear, the downhearted to be restored, the hopeless to have hope, the lost to find their way, the oppressed to be released, the possessed to be free through the power of an almighty God who cares about their every need.

The same God who cared enough about you and me to send someone our way: someone who was faithful to Jesus Christ, the call of God, and the Great Commission. May you and I never forget where God brought us from, and may we seek him more each day for the anointing of God that breaks every yoke and allows us the honor of sharing the Gospel.

As an itinerant minister, you should graciously receive whatever is given to you by the church or pastor. Many larger churches give set honorariums while smaller churches seem to give beyond their means. But whatever the amount, you must realize that God will be the final judge on what happens behind the scenes in order for you to receive your check. You may not know all that a church has gone through, or that the pastor alone has given the monies because the church does not have the funds to pay you. Whatever the amount, give God praise and allow God to be a blessing to others through you, and you will be blessed of God at the next location. There are times when every one of us can sense the need to "sow" instead of reap. God will undoubtedly bless you for your attentive ear to his call and obedience to his word.

A pastor shared with me one time that although they were not a very large church, they had flown a special speaker in for revival services.

They had taken care of the accommodations, rental vehicle, spending money, fuel, as well as a very gracious offering for the Sunday through Wednesday services. The offering was probably two to three times what an evangelist would normally get for a Sunday through Wednesday series of meetings, and this individual said that he was "pretty disappointed" with the offering.

When I heard that, I must admit my anger began to rage. Those kinds of people don't need to be in ministry if they only have a business mentality. This person had forgotten all that God had blessed him with during his early days and the need to exemplify graciousness in giving, whether extending an invitation to give or receiving from someone else. God's favor will undoubtedly be with those endeavoring to be his devoted representatives—even in giving.

STAYING IN THE PASTOR'S HOME

Perhaps you are very good friends with a pastor who only has a basement apartment or spare room for you. This is not the best scenario, but one that can be a sincere blessing to the church—helping keep expenses low—as well as a blessing to the pastor. You may offer to pay for a hotel or motel yourself depending on the size of the community or rent an RV if that would make you more comfortable. However, if you do find yourself in this type of situation, you should be sensitive to several aspects of staying in a pastor's home.

First, do your best to avoid being in the house alone with the opposite gender. If you are a man and the male pastor has errands or visits to make, you should plan on either joining the pastor in these visits or ask to be let off at the church so that you can study and pray while the pastor is gone. If you have your own transportation, ensure that you leave the house at the same time as the pastor. The same procedure should be followed if you are a woman. Remove any possibility for gossip or rumors to flourish about you and your relationship with anyone in the pastor's home.

Second, keep food demands to a minimum—if at all. Be sensitive to the cost of food and recall Proverbs 23:2, "and put a knife to your throat if you are given to gluttony." You should eat whatever is put in front of you if at all possible. Let your host know of any allergies or special diet concerns you have, or that anyone with you has, early on before he or she begins cooking. If there are certain snacks you enjoy, ensure that you purchase them yourself prior to arrival.

Third, don't take advantage of your host's hospitality. That includes taking lengthy showers or indulging in their foods, snacks or specialty items that have not been offered to you. Some church leaders provide a food or snack basket for you, but don't expect this. Joyfully receive what you are offered if possible. Keep any music or noise from your room to a minimum.

Fourth, clean up after yourself and take care of your own personal needs. You should make your bed every day and keep your room clean. Rinse out the bathtub and wipe down the sink when you have finished showering, shaving, or brushing your teeth. Hang up your towels and re-use them if possible. If you have laundry needs, ask about local laundromats instead of just taking it for granted that you can use a host's washer and dryer. If you use their ironing board and iron, make sure you put these items away when you finish. These actions reflect an attitude of appreciation to your host and give the proper courtesy that you would like if you had a guest in your home.

Finally, be sensitive to schedules. Are the host pastors bi-vocational? Are children in the home? Do they have to leave for school at a certain time? What time do they normally have breakfast, lunch or dinner? When are showers or baths normally taken? Make sure that you allow those household members to go about their routines without interruption, and you will be known as a great guest to have. It is also nice to help out whenever the opportunity arises. Volunteer to do little odd jobs around the house or help with the dishes after meals. At the very least, be ready to take your own dishes to the kitchen and remember to thank your host for the little things they did to make your stay enjoyable.

All this to say, as a guest you should be as unnoticeable as possible. When you leave, the pastor and his or her spouse should be surprised at how well you have left things. This helps create a positive experience and opens a wider door of opportunity for ministry in the future. Your actions will also be retold to other ministers in the area so be a great guest! Once you depart, you might prayerfully consider having some flowers or some other small gift sent to the pastor's wife for all the meals and efforts that were given on your behalf.

DEALING WITH DISHONEST PEOPLE

No matter who you are, after a time you will cross paths with folks who are less than honest. Some people are downright liars, and some of those folks actually stand behind pulpits of churches across this entire globe. People are people, and not everyone who answers the call of God to be a Christian or spiritual leader is a pristine reflection of Jesus Christ. As a matter of fact, God is still working on all of us; and we all can use improvement in one area or another.

When calling pastors for service opportunities, I have heard responses like:

"I'm booked up for the year."

"We're in the middle of remodeling right now, and the budget can't handle guest speakers."

"Can you send me some material?"

I have had other church leaders tell me to call them because they want to have me come, and then they won't take my calls or return the phone calls in which I'm able to leave a voice mail or an actual message with a secretary.

So, what does an evangelist do who feels God has truly called him or her? As one veteran evangelist told me once: "Marshall, you always take the high road." He meant that we must not allow others who are dishonest and hurtful to bring us down to their level of character. When you run into folks like this, you just must move on and leave them behind. Their lack of character and integrity will catch up with them, but our responsibility is to pray for them and leave them in God's hand. He is the judge, and He alone knows what can bring them back to a right relationship with Him.

I must admit that I struggled with this aspect of ministry when I first started. I thought that I would have a wonderful time ministering to God's people and have some great fellowship with the church leaders. But through the years, I have discovered that there are church leaders who are worldlier than those outside the church. The local church isn't full of perfect people or perfect leaders—we're all striving to do our best to pay our bills, share the love of Jesus Christ the best way we know how, and make it to Heaven when Jesus decides to take us home.

When those people you look up to or who are in leadership hurt you, the only option we have is to take the hurt of betrayal to the cross. God has called us to be men and women of prayer because it is in God's presence where mountains are moved, people are changed, and healing takes place. I pray you never experience some of the hurtful things I've walked through over the years. But this I know: whatever you must walk through, Jesus Christ will walk through it with you if you let Him. I pray that you will, if you haven't already, experience the realization of his nearness—because it will change the way you do ministry. Your effectiveness in ministry doesn't depend on your talents but on the presence and goodness of God Himself.

AN ENCOURAGING WORD
ON DIVERSITY

The following is an email that I wrote in response to a fellow evangelist's inquiry about ministry. I pray that it might encourage you in some small way.

Timothy,[13]

In pondering your dilemma, I'm reminded of what the Lord keeps telling me - "remember what I called you to do." I have run into the same situations as you, and it does not mean that certain folks are wrong and you are right. I don't necessarily agree with everything I see on the ministry landscape either, but I have to believe that those folks who are more seeker focused are praying for God's guidance and direction just like we are. I can't worry about all those people who don't like evangelists or have quit having Sunday evening and mid-week services. A lot of those folks have been burned by evangelists, and it will take a lot of time and God's nudging to change their minds.

One thing that has helped me more than anything has been prayer and fasting. I truly seek God's favor and anointing as I prayerfully call pastors and conduct services. You are who you are and whatever the ministry focus God has given you will bear witness by others. Yes, I too have friends that won't let me come to their church, but I just leave that to God and try to be the best friend that they have whenever we get together. I just try to maintain a humble attitude and serve the best I can as the Lord opens doors. It is HIS ministry, and whenever He starts closing doors of opportunity, then I will know that as I fast and pray, it may be God's timing of a new season of ministry in my life, whatever that may be.

The financial hardships have caused many to become bi-vocational or conduct ministry while their spouse works. With my education,

---

13 Not his real name

I've been blessed to incorporate some teaching at Bible schools, as well as seminars to help equip churches in evangelism. God uses us a lot in healing and altar ministry with prophecy at times. It's all about humbling ourselves before God and allowing Him to guide our steps.

God has planted you where you are, and I'm sure He wants to use you in that region of the country. The current trend isn't necessarily favorable to evangelists, but God doesn't call us without opening doors ... even with other denominations and fellowships. What are your gifts and talents? Are there additional ministry opportunities that you could incorporate into your ministry - i.e. school assemblies, outreach clinics, leadership. God can use all of these and more (as you well know).

I've seen the self-help seminars and all the coaching resources available today, but God has dealt with me about seeking Him first and focusing on an anointed ministry whenever the opportunity affords itself. I still believe that people are hungry for a timely Word from God that speaks to their hearts. There is an old saying that "ministry makes room for itself." When there is a visible anointing word gets around about it. If God wants me to go to seminars or coaching events, I'll go, but I just want Him to guide me in it all. I have seen a majority of my friends incorporate their ministries in order to provide an avenue for friends and family who want to support their ministries financially. I don't encourage young ministers in this, but you've been in ministry for several years, and this might be a means to help you in those lean times when services are few. It's just something to pray about - let God lead you!

As you've undoubtedly heard, the methods change, but the message stays the same. There may be ways to package your ministry that could make it more appealing to folks in your area who are more seeker oriented. I love old-time Pentecost, but I love connecting to the unchurched seeker as well. I need God's sensitivity to help me connect with the differing congregations I encounter. If church leaders and planters no longer want Pentecost or Sunday night services, they will have to answer to God for their decisions. You and I must focus on maintaining a servant attitude and hearing from God for direction and ministry as we strive to follow His calling.

I'm not sure if I helped at all, but I do understand where you are coming from, Timothy. It can be extremely discouraging and frustrating at the same time. But as my friends have told me more than once - it's all about the call. God called us, and He will keep us in this calling of the evangelist. Even when we must work part-time or find other ways to help us stay on the field - it's about the call. We're not responsible for what other folks do - just for how we respond to God's call upon our lives.

Again, this may not have helped at all, but I'd be happy to chat if you like...just give me a shout on my cell tomorrow sometime. May the favor of God rest upon you and your ministry in the years ahead, and may the Holy Spirit of God give you crystal clear direction in your specific situation. Thanks SO MUCH for sharing your concerns with me and I will continue praying for you and all our evangelists as we follow the call.

Blessings,

Marshall

TRAVELING WITH FAMILY

Being able to take our children with us as we traveled has been one of the greatest joys that Nancy and I have had over the years. Exposing Joshua and Hannah to so many interesting people and situations over the years has given them a breadth of wisdom that most young people do not have. Yes, there have been some challenges, but they have all been opportunities to grow. As our children grew they became involved in ministry and shared the responsibilities with us; but early on there were some trying—but hilarious now—moments with our children. The following paragraphs may help you if you have children accompanying you as you travel.

Discipline

You will find out early on that everyone watches you and especially how you discipline your children. Many folks love to give advice (some of them do not even have children), so always be gracious and show appreciation for their insights. But as the Lord would have it, you will probably need to discipline a child while in the presence of others and occasionally you may need to do this while you are in the middle of preaching! That is very humbling indeed!

When our oldest son, Joshua, was around five years old, we had a service at a smaller church. Joshua was continually making noise and causing distractions as only a five-year-old can. About halfway through my message I called Joshua to come up to the front row and sit down. Now, if attention was Joshua's goal he probably got more than he bargained for! But the truth is, young children will be children, and their attention span is even shorter than adults. Not only Joshua, but everyone in that church knew that Joshua better not do anything except be the ideal child while sitting on the front row during my sermon—and we were consistent in our discipline.

Book Bag

Our family enjoys books and Nancy always had a bag of books when we traveled to help keep the children preoccupied. These books were cheaply acquired at sales and thrift stores (see Chapter 7 on cutting costs). Nancy had coloring books, picture books and other "quiet" toys that would keep the children quiet during our regular service. Nancy would often sit on the back row in smaller churches in order to minimize the distraction of any activity.

As you travel, you will find others who want to help you and may notice the books and puzzles you might have brought along with you. You also may find gifts awaiting you during special times at these wonderful churches. I've even heard of smaller churches celebrating Christmas with their guest speakers and showering them with gifts.

God's people still hear from God, and it is absolutely amazing to see God's hand of provision when you least expect it!

Lastly, you will want to continually refresh that bag, switch out coloring books, picture books, puzzles, and toys. Just make sure that any toys you bring are quiet ones that will not cause distractions for whoever is preaching.

Doing What's Best For Your Children

Although this seems to go without saying, there will be times in your ministry when you will not feel comfortable about leaving your child or children in a church's children ministry area. I always trusted Nancy's intuition about those things, and whenever a less-than-comfortable feeling arose, we just kept our children with us—even during Sunday School. We never tried to be offensive; we just said: "Thank you, but we'll just keep so-and-so with us." No explanation is needed or offered; we just stated that the children would be with us.

If God has entrusted you with children to raise up in the fear and admonition of the Lord, do not hesitate to do whatever is best for them in your differing situations. There are many wonderful churches and children's workers helping with God's work today, so do not let a few less-than-sterling folks persuade you differently. However, you must face the reality that not everyone you meet in church will be a positive experience for you or your child. You will also run into situations where there are no volunteers to staff a children's ministry in that particular church. When you come prepared, even if the worst happens, you and your family will still be prepared to share the wonderful Gospel of Jesus Christ with that congregation.

Family Fun On The Road

As you travel the highways and byways, you will have the opportunity to see more interesting landmarks, cities, and national parks than you can imagine. You may think that driving for hours on end would be extremely boring—and it can be—but there are wonderful surprises and many great people that we have seen over the years. My children are much richer for it and have a worldview that extends beyond our local community. There are many fun family activities that you can do "on the road" and your creativity is the only limiting factor! One evangelist shared this with me years ago:

> At the risk of stating the obvious (as if preachers are afraid of THAT) when my kids were small (and even now that it is just myself and my wife traveling) and we had some extra travel time, we enjoyed just popping in on historic sites. Usually, these were state parks which were free or very inexpensive, and designated by a brown sign along the highway. It was fun to see one and just yell 'Hey, how about we check out the Battle of Horseshoe Bend?' We saw stuff ranging from Civil War and Indian battlegrounds to a CCC museum. My kids developed an interest in history and were able to add first-hand input to class discussions in school, which made them feel special and 'well-traveled.'[14]

It seems that national parks, caves, and seashores were among the top hits with our children over the years. We are all book fans too, so there were many times when a good book inside on hot or rainy days was just the thing to make everyone happy! Since we also have this strange attraction to good food, we have had the pleasure of eating some great ice cream, BBQ, fried chicken, chicken fried steak, and well—you get the idea—lots of good food at so many wonderful places in America and abroad.

It's The Little Things

Keeping your marriage and family happy when you are in ministry can be challenging—and when you are in itinerant ministry it can be more challenging! Over the years, I have noticed that it seems like the little things I did out of thoughtfulness to my wife were appreciated more than things that were expensive. If you have never read "The Five

---

14 Many thanks to Tim Collins for sharing his own family's experience.

Love Languages" by Gary Chapman or "Love and Respect" by Emerson Eggerichs, I would highly recommend them to you. Find ways to spend time with your spouse and children—it will keep your marriage and family healthy and provide a hedge around your ministry. Most of these little things that I am talking about just took time, which is how some people really spell love—T-I-M-E.

Doing things around the house unexpectedly (like helping to wash the dishes, vacuum, making the bed, etc.), as well as special notes hidden where only my wife would find them (haven't done that in a while—but need to), were always appreciated. I also enjoyed getting her some flowers once a month if possible. I used to go to a local ALDI's grocery store and get six roses for $3.19! You may have discount stores close by, and when the folks at the checkout counter ask you what you did wrong, you can just tell them that you are buying some cheap insurance for a great marriage!

When on the road by myself, I talk with my wife and even the children once or twice a day. I always call and pray with the kids before service and give a service report to Nancy. Then, I have prayer time afterward with Nancy for evening services, because she prays for me while I am away ministering. She also likes to know what God did during the service.

Modern technology now allows us to communicate via Skype, FaceTime, and other venues, no matter where we are around the globe. There is no excuse for not staying in touch with those you love when you're on the road. I even have a phone card in case there is no cell phone or Internet reception where I am holding services.

At the risk of being redundant with my "write notes" comment above; that is something my wife appreciates almost more than anything else. She can't be with me on many trips, but once I sent her a "thinking of you" card with a personal note inside. I think she would rather get a hand-written love note from me than flowers—because I took time to write mushy stuff down. That's not always the easiest thing for men to do, but it is definitely appreciated by most wives. I'm sure the opposite is true as well for ladies who travel. My wife still has notes that I wrote to her years ago. HINT: you don't have to be away from family to write a note either...

OFFERINGS, TAXES, AND TITHES

Here is a copy of an email that was sent to me, as well as my response. Richard Hammar, the current legal counsel for the General Council of the Assemblies of God, concurred.

"My name is #####, and I am a licensed minister with the ##### District, I am also listed as a national evangelist with the A/G. I have a Question about receiving offerings or honorariums from the church. Can you tell me if there is a certain amount that is not tax deductible? For example, I was told that if I received from one church less than 500 dollars, then I did not have to file taxes for that. Also, would I have to file taxes for any money at the end of the year that isn't tax deductible? Thanks very much."

Here was my response ...

"Brother #####, We always direct legal and tax questions to our General Council legal counsel, Richard Hammar. You are more than welcome to call him here at our National Leadership and Resource Center.

As far as general reporting measures, all income should be used when calculating tithes. Non-receipted cash gifts by individuals are usually not reported for tax purposes since the individual giving you the cash gift is already paying taxes on that money. Any checks received from churches should be reported, and any checks $600 and over should have an IRS Form 1099-MISC issued by the church so you will need to ensure they have a signed IRS Form W-9 from you. These are just general guidelines for individuals, so please make sure that you confirm these and other items with your personal CPA and/ or Richard Hammar, especially if you are incorporated as a 501(c)3."

As an additional note, if you are a nonprofit, many ministers that I have talked with consider all offerings to the organization as monies to pay that organization's expenses for ministry. As I briefly mentioned earlier, the money you tithe on in that situation would be the money that the nonprofit organization pays you as a salary. The organization is seen as being the ministry that God has called you to serve, and the monies given to it are God's way of funding that ministry to which God has called you. You still need to fill out and file all tax-associated paperwork required by federal and state governments, and you may have special guidelines from your fellowship or denomination that must be taken into consideration as well.

Nonprofit Organization

Some evangelists take steps to incorporate their ministry as a nonprofit organization. Since every state has slightly different laws and procedures for incorporating and operating a non-profit organization, you should check with some local legal counsel and your state's Secretary of State for the appropriate application procedures and reports required in the United States. You may also want to enlist the help of a local Certified Public Accountant (CPA) who is well-versed in nonprofit accounting and who might be willing to help you for a nominal fee. Other countries will have their own guidelines, and you should reference those if you live in another country or desire to base your corporation there. Once incorporated, your non-profit organization can receive gifts from supporters that are tax-deductible for the giver in the United States. This is the primary advantage of the nonprofit organization. Another advantage is that your ministry is clearly kept separate from your personal finances and is operated as a normal business.

The organization does not pay tithes or taxes but pays you a salary, which you tithe on and pay taxes from. Many evangelists have told me that this helps them through slow times of the year when the schedule isn't quite as full—especially during holidays and special national events. So, I asked the following question of some evangelists: "What are the pros and cons of incorporation & becoming a non-profit organization as an evangelistic ministry?" Here are a few of the responses that I received.

"I became a nonprofit corporation in the early 80s. I have found no disadvantages to it as far as I am concerned. In fact, it seems to be a great advantage in many ways."

"We've been on both sides of this issue. The nonprofit adds considerable complexity to your accounting. Its major advantage is that you can issue tax receipts for donors. Our limited experience has been that if you don't need to give tax receipts, don't mess with the expense and additional paperwork."

I have talked to numerous evangelist friends who have incorporated their ministries and have found it to be an advantage for them. However, you must realize when you first begin in evangelistic ministry your supporters may be few and far between! That said you should wait until you sense God's confirmation of the ministry and you have been on the field for a few years before undertaking the expense of incorporating.

Our family was in evangelistic ministry for almost seventeen years before we finally felt the Lord leading us to incorporate—definitely longer than most evangelists. However, we were able to start a missions' account with the Assemblies of God's World Missions department early in our ministry for churches and individuals who wanted to support our missions' work. All of our other activities stateside were able to help us with our day-to-day living expenses. Other denominational organizations may have similar avenues in place to help those getting started in itinerant ministry, so it is definitely worth your time to investigate that possibility.

In talking with one evangelist, he felt that incorporating would protect him from any potential lawsuits. While I hope that no evangelist ever finds himself or herself in that predicament, our legal counsel shared that anybody can be sued. Incorporating does not guarantee protection from legal action. We live in a litigious society today in the United States and the best defense against a lawsuit is to stay in the perfect will of God as we strive to emulate Jesus Christ. If you live in other countries, you will need to abide by the letter of the law where you live. As Christ stated in Luke 20:25, "He said to them, 'Then render to Caesar the things that are Caesar's, and to God the things that are God's.'"

Financial accountability is another benefit of a nonprofit organization. The accountant who helps you can set up a system for providing a housing allowance for you, as well as any other benefits the ministry may provide—like contributions to a 403 (b) retirement account. Contributions to this type of retirement account must be from ministry income only. As I shared, the fine line of distinction between your personal finances and the ministry can be advantageous in maintaining integrity and accountability for the organization. This is due, in part, because the incorporated ministry is seen as a separate entity in the eyes of the government.

The ministry can hire employees and issue tax forms when needed whether you are incorporated or not, but expenses incurred for the ministry—like meals—can be reimbursed. You will need to apply for an Employer Identification Number (EIN) for tax reporting purposes, which can be done prior to incorporating if you have employees. An EIN is also helpful if you want to keep from using your social security number on W-9 forms. Churches usually request a W-9 when you receive $600 or more in honorariums.

The cost of incorporating as a nonprofit arises as a major challenge and most evangelists don't realize how fast these expenses can multiply. Since the IRS in the United States sees the nonprofit corporation as a separate entity, a separate tax return must be completed and filed in addition to your personal tax return. There are some CPA groups that specialize in nonprofit tax preparation that may give discounts.

Additionally, it pays to check with other evangelists on who they use. Many nonprofit organizations use accounting firms that do not reside in their state, so don't hesitate to do your homework and find someone that will work for your benefit.

There are also fees involved with incorporating: the initial incorporation fees, as well as yearly fees and a nonprofit application fee to the Internal

Revenue Service. The initial accounting Form 1023, Application for Recognition of Exemption Under Section 501(c)3, may cost several hundred to over a thousand dollars for someone to help you fill out. You also have a filing fee based on income now with the IRS. You may be able to submit a Form 1023EZ if you qualify, which currently costs $400.

Check with your accountant and the IRS for current fees before you apply. You will also need to budget for annual board meetings and a Form 990 every year. Some accountants may charge around $1,000 (or hopefully less) to help you file this. If you have employees, you will need to file the appropriate paperwork for any withholding from salaries.

Most evangelists, who contemplate incorporating as a nonprofit, only think about providing an avenue for supporters to contribute and receive a tax-deductible receipt for their gifts. However, as you can see above, there are numerous expenses that come with incorporating. It pays to "count the cost," as Jesus shared with his disciples in Luke 14:28. You need to know that the Lord is leading you to incorporate your ministry and that you have enough revenue from supporters and ministry activities to warrant incorporating. Do your homework and read up on what will be required of you after you incorporate in your state. There are numerous websites that promote themselves as being helpful in this regard.

CONDUCTING OUTREACH MINISTRY

Although many evangelists do multiple types of ministry, local community outreach still stands as one critical aid you can give to the local church. After all, as Ephesians 4:12 states, all the ministry gifts are: "to equip the saints for the work of ministry, for building up the body of Christ." Most people in the church are apprehensive about sharing their faith in a community that has increased in its hostility towards Christians. Working to embolden the church community for outreach can have different approaches that utilize relational, invitational, intellectual, and confrontational evangelism.

Community Outreach

Working with a church in community outreach usually embraces the invitational evangelism model wherein a team works together in one housing area or neighborhood that can be canvased in one to two hours. You will need a team effort to make this truly effective. Adding a free meal and/or clothing give away helps increase the appeal to area residents. Try to do a little homework prior to the outreach to see if you can determine the ages of those in the neighborhood and their socioeconomic level. Then plan accordingly. Having some suitable sound equipment and a worship team that can play the style of music that can connect with the local people is vital.

Saturday seems to be the best day for outreach with a start time around mid-morning. That will give folks enough time to cook the food and invite the neighborhood to your event. Check with the local pastor on any permits needed for the outreach and then plan for your team to arrive early that morning to set up. Once the rest of the church arrives, give them some concrete examples of what they might say and how they might respond to inquiries. Always encourage the people to ask if there is anything they can pray with the people about and send them out in groups of at least two people. There is a biblical precedent by Jesus Christ that we base this on as he sent his disciples out two-by-two.

Plan for a variety of speakers initially since you do not know whether you will have children only, youth, adults, or a variety of people attending the worship time and presentation of the Gospel. Some benevolent organizations even have a short service first and then invite those in attendance to join them for the food and any clothing or toy giveaways. Make sure you have ample resources to give anyone who makes a decision for Christ or would just like to read more about this Christ you are preaching about. Give away Bibles and other instructional material as the opportunity presents itself.

I worked with one home missionary in the United States who partnered with the city of St. Louis that was having a local community outreach to the homeless. Many of the homeless there were veterans and so many local organizations came together to provide free haircuts, clothing, backpacks, legal advice, and other services that would benefit the homeless. The missionary set up a prayer tent in the middle of the other organizations, and we were able to minister to many folks who stopped by our tent. It was a great way to help a church build a good reputation within its own community when it is seen as a partner that helps its local community.

An evangelist serves as a coach and teacher in this type of situation. Since there is some anxiety surrounding outreach—even for Pentecostals—a person who is passionate about outreach can help allay many unfounded fears. Partnering up people for outreach is also a great way to help people see that they can do what the Lord Jesus Christ has commanded us in the Great Commission (Matthew 28:16-20; Mark 16:14-18; Luke 24:44-49; John 20: 19-23; Acts 1:4-8).

The Lord taught me a valuable lesson when I was helping with a community outreach in the New Orleans area one year during Mardi Gras. For some reason, I took off by myself to invite folks to the free food and clothing giveaway that our ministry was hosting. At one home, I met Monroe, who had a scar over the top of his head—from one ear to the other. He had some speech issues, but after I asked him if there was anything I could pray with him about, he began to tell me how he watched a certain television preacher every morning and prayed for those in his neighborhood.

Monroe began to pray for me, and I just began weeping, as his passionate prayer seemed to invoke something from Heaven. We chatted a bit more afterward, and I invited him to the outreach. While I was walking back to the outreach area, the Holy Spirit seemed to say to me: "See, you thought you came out here to minister to these people, but I used them to minister to you." The Lord reminded me that he was just looking for a willing vessel—one that he could use—and bless at the most unexpected time.

Mardi Gras Outreach

While working on this chapter I had the privilege of joining some friends for a special Mardi Gras outreach. To say that this type of outreach is not for the meek would be an understatement. The assault against the Christian can be intimidating and extremely vulgar. People are usually intoxicated, and many are on drugs of one kind or another. Prostitution is in full swing, and the homeless are looking for a handout wherever they can find one. The police are in full force these days, but often, fights break out and are over before law enforcement arrives on the scene.

With all these hindrances, one might ask why in the world would you want to witness or preach to drunken people on Bourbon Street, Jackson Square, or any of the side streets nearby during the height of Mardi Gras? What effect do you think it is really going to have? As a matter of fact, I had several people on the street ask me this! One man said that it was just wrong for us even to be there with all the scandalous activities.

But didn't Jesus Christ tell us that His followers were to be "salt and light" (Matthew 5:13-16) even as he stated His own role as the "light of the world (John 8:12)?" Even in the midst of a very dark place God has called us all to shine His light (Matthew 5:16). I cannot tell you how many people left Mardi Gras thinking about God and the possibility of a relationship with Him. I also cannot tell you how many people I talked with or witnessed to who had experienced a terrible injustice at the hands of Christians. Too often, I found myself apologizing for the wrongs of others who had abused the Scriptures—solely for the opportunity to share the hope of Christ.

One thing I realized early in the outreach was the need for a command of Scripture. By that I mean you must have either memorized relevant Scriptures or have them easily marked in a Bible that you don't mind having abused. It is the Scripture that will not return void (Isaiah 55:11) and God's Word, which Jesus said was "sharper than any two-edged sword" (Hebrews 4:12). The cross is offensive to those who don't know

Christ, but that does not mean that Christians need to be intentionally offensive. We must share the full counsel of God with His love for those who do not know Him; then allow the Holy Spirit and God's word to perform any needed surgery.

The reason you need to know your Scripture is because you will run into every kind of religious and moral belief under the sun. There were Hindus, atheists, Muslims, backslidden Christians, homosexuals, lesbians, warlocks, witches, prostitutes, and a host of other religious and moral views represented at Mardi Gras. No one can know everything about every religion, and many will try to question you concerning your own experience. That's why you must know the Word of God. Scripture will cause people to think and sense the Holy Spirit's conviction—even in the middle of Mardi Gras or any other festivity.

One concern I had prior to our outreach arose from my prior military schooling and service. I prayed a lot about how I would handle reproach from others who might be belligerent and confrontational. The Lord gave me a great lesson on the third night of our outreach. I had a young man who was drunk approach me and call me a derogatory name. He repeated it a couple of times, and I didn't say a thing. I was bigger than he was and knew he was just trying to upset me. Then, he took some of my tracks that I was handing out and tore them up and threw them on the ground—right before his friend came up and pulled him away. Well, I thought: "Welcome to Mardi Gras ministry!"

But at that moment, I realized that God was right in the middle of the entire confrontation. I felt as though a wall of God's grace and protection were upon me. I did not get mad or respond in a derogatory manner. I just kept quiet and let him talk. It reminded me of Ephesians 6:12, which shares how our battle is not against flesh and blood but against "spiritual wickedness." When God calls us to take the Gospel to a dark place, He is faithful to walk with us—even when we suffer reprimand or even physical retaliation.

This leads me to an important point. When God's calls you to conduct a special outreach in spiritually dark places, don't go out by yourself unless you truly feel a divine directive to do so. In our outreach, there were about fifty people from our group on the street witnessing and preaching at any one time. Numerous other Christian organizations were also on the street, so we had a great host of like-minded folks in the middle of a decadent festival.

When doing a major outreach over several days, you must have a schedule. Our outreach schedule went something like this: Breakfast 7:30 to 8:30 a.m.; Worship time 10:30 a.m.; Lunch 12:30 to 1:30 p.m.; Ministry time 2 to 4:30 p.m. (French Quarter / Neighborhood outreach); Dinner 5:30 to 6:30 p.m.; Worship time 7 to 8 p.m.; Midnight French Quarter (Bourbon Street) 9 to midnight.

As you can see, our schedule left plenty of time to take care of personal needs around meal times, but the days were long! I don't think I ever got to bed before 2 a.m. and I only got about four hours of sleep a night! Special festival outreaches are not for the faint of heart. That's why the worship times were so crucial prior to going out for ministry. If you lead a team to special festival outreaches, ensure you have a great team in place and plan well ahead in order to try and cover every possible need.

When you preach in this type of setting, you tend to preach more of a shotgun-type message that has lots of salvation Scripture. You are trying to preach to most people who do not want you around. We had lesbians come up in front of the speaker and begin to kiss and raise their middle finger to those close by. Then they started embracing and rubbing each other to flaunt their sexual orientation—all while the preacher was speaking. So, be prepared for the unexpected and stay focused on sharing the Gospel message of Jesus Christ. The Word of God will not return void. You may not see it—but you must claim that Scripture repeatedly.

Age-based, Vocational, and Special Interest Outreaches

If you help lead outreaches in local schools, nursing homes, or other age-based communities, you need to do your homework. Check with other evangelists who conduct school assemblies, collegiate or other age oriented events. School assemblies are high energy, and you must adhere to the local school's policies regarding what is permissible to share and what is not. Many times, in school assemblies, God cannot be mentioned, but character- and moral-based presentations are allowed. Invitations to special evening events where the Gospel is preached are often the norm.

When working with college level students a more academic approach may be preferred. Check with local ministries like Chi Alpha that may be able to help you in your outreach approach. You may also want to actually partner with these organizations in order to build rapport with organizations on campus and foster a Kingdom-minded approach to ministry on campus. This may provide further invitations to partner with them for on-campus events whereby the church could provide funding or resources to help support annual events where the Gospel is presented, and the church is recognized for its partnership. It is always best when you can work with existing organizations.

Some vocational or special ministry outreaches may involve public servants, businesses, prison or military personnel in a community. Whenever possible, see if there are chaplains already working in these areas and marshal their support and counsel on specific needs you and your team could help fill. This is especially critical in working with military or other government personnel. There are policies in place that cannot be overlooked and the men and women chaplains who serve these folks will know what is permissible and what is not. As you gain respect by those leaders as someone who adheres to proper protocol, you will find more open doors and invitations to partner with these chaplains for additional ministry opportunities.

GIVING THE CHURCH
BACK TO THE PASTOR

Giving the church back to the pastor is one of the greatest things an evangelist can do when a series of services comes to completion. This small courtesy is usually completed prior to preaching your message on the last night of your time with that congregation. You should openly thank the pastor for allowing you the privilege of sharing the Gospel with his or her congregation and charge every person in that congregation to support their pastor and undergird him or her, their spouse and family in prayer after you leave. Showing this appreciation for the opportunity to minister in that church is always appropriate and usually valued more than you realize.

This allows you the opportunity to not only show appreciation, but also to publicly let the pastor and congregation know that you are not looking for a church to pastor. On rare occasions, a guest speaker has come in and contributed to part of a larger problem. You should strive to add value to that local church and never have problems associated with your name. Oftentimes, the last thing people see and hear from you will be what they remember long after you are gone.

DON'T TAKE YOURSELF
TOO SERIOUSLY

We all will make mistakes over the years of ministry and forget different items as we pack for ministry in some far away city or state. The attitude with which we traverse these times will make for some great memories if we handle it in the right way. Taking your mistakes out on those closest to you or allowing them to affect your ministry negatively will only hinder what God wants to do in that situation. You must remember that the enemy of your soul will use every tactic available and that includes forgetfulness, pride, and anger.

Many years ago, when I was just starting out as an evangelist, our family had the opportunity for ministry in a small, rural church. The congregation there had become a second family to us over the years, and our visits there always helped remind me of where we started from and the real reason God called us to ministry in the first place. These people were always so genuine and down-to-earth. Their simplicity of life always reminded me that most folks in the world today are just trying to live life the best way they know how and pay their bills.

As I was dressing for the service I made a horrifying discovery—I had forgotten to pack my dress shoes! I looked high and low to see if I was somehow mistaken, but the truth glared me in the face. I had forgotten my shoes. The only pair of shoes that I had with me was a pair of work boots. I was livid with anger over the fact that I did not have any dress shoes and almost took my anger out on my family.

Normally, I pack as I visualize dressing for a service and start at the top: undershirt, underwear, shirt, tie, tie chain, suit, belt, socks, shoes, and Bible. I'm pretty sure ladies have their own method of packing, but my visualization method usually helps me pack everything I need. But somehow on this trip, I had forgotten shoes.

As I sat and contemplated whether to run to the store and buy a new pair, I realized that no stores were open at that time of day where I was ministering. I also realized that skipping the service was not an option. I finally concluded that I just had to swallow my pride and wear my work boots with my suit. I know you're probably laughing out loud right now, but it was no laughing matter to me then! However, by the time I got to the church I was laughing at my predicament. When I got up to preach, I had to show off my nice work boots to the congregation. They laughed right along with me, and God really touched quite a few folks that morning despite the guest speaker forgetting his dress shoes.

I share all that to say that there may be times when God wants to give you a very large dose of humility. The Scriptures tell us in Proverbs 18:12 (ESV) that "humility comes before honor." Jesus modeled humility throughout his entire ministry. He was born in a stable, endured the shame of crucifixion, and paid a debt for our sins that he did not owe.

I have encountered prolific speakers who think quite highly of themselves, but that do not embody the ministry of Jesus Christ. I applaud those ministers who have risen to magnificent platforms of influence. Their level of accountability before God is huge and their ministries often touch millions of people. But whenever God allows something humbling to happen in your ministry, don't allow the enemy to win by getting angry and taking your anger out on your staff or loved ones. Realize that God has given you an opportunity to see Him work despite all your efforts. Additionally, find a little humor in your situation—and realize it will make for a great story later in life if you don't take yourself too seriously.

SUMMARY

Although one could talk a lifetime about the many different situations someone might encounter in ministry, I hope that these things I've shared will help you at some point. The most important thing you can do is continue to hear from Heaven so that your counsel is from God himself; and foster friendships among other evangelists and pastors whom you can call for advice when unfamiliar situations arise. After all our years of ministry, I still call my friends on occasion with questions about situations that I have never experienced. Proverbs 11:14b tells us: "In an abundance of counselors there is safety." With our ever-changing culture and societal needs, we need all the wisdom available to us in order to impact people who need Christ.

CHAPTER 7

Downtime
and Promotion

(A QUESTION AND ANSWER SESSION)

Downtime and promotion are a part of our ministry as evangelists. Concerning downtime, you may have some open weekends or meetings that get canceled—along with days between meetings when you are not ministering. As a self-employed itinerant minister or any kind of evangelistic ministry, these seasons of extended non-ministry time arise, and you need to be productive during those free days. You need to guard the important areas of your life and be proactive in adding value to your ministry. Invest in yourself and develop or strengthen the ministry so that you can take it to a higher level of effectiveness.

Downtime often includes working on the promotional aspects of your ministry. Promotion should be tasteful, professional, and accurate. Exaggerations in ministry are not helpful in the long run and only cut your ministry short at best. In this chapter, I'll share some thoughts on guarding different aspects of your ministry and using your downtime effectively. I'll also cover some different areas of promotion that are cost-effective along with some pitfalls to avoid.

GUARD YOUR STUDY TIME

One of the most important things you can do is to guard your study time. You must keep the proverbial blade sharp. When we begin to preach old messages, they start making us complacent. If we're not careful, we will get lazy and say, "Okay Lord, which one of the messages that I have already crafted do you want me to preach this time?" As a minister of the Gospel, you must adopt a different mindset that seeks a fresh word from God every week. After all, a pastor often must have a new message two to three times every week! That's a lot of hard work, and as an evangelist, you may need a series of messages. If you're in a Sunday through Wednesday revival meeting, you will need five messages. Those fresh messages often come through your daily Bible study time. Guard that time by every means possible because that is the lifeline of your ministry.

Oftentimes the Lord will help you by providing a fresh word from Him when you wake up early in the morning. The Lord may burden you and prompt you to write the very message that you will use that night. But, it doesn't always work that way. Whether the Lord gives you a fresh message for a service or He has burdened you to preach a message that you preached before; we shouldn't be content preaching our old messages. We should always be pressing in and trying to hear from Heaven and have a fresh word for the people to whom we are speaking. I read a quote by John Wesley that reflects this mindset: "Once in seven years I burn all my sermons; for it is a shame if I cannot write better sermons now than I did seven years ago."

Sometimes we joke about all the challenges and distractions of ministry. Thankfully, God knows how to prompt us and help us through even the most difficult days. The day my computer crashed, and I lost all my old messages and research work ranks right up there as one of the worst ministry tragedies of my life.

However, when we go through our daily routines and try to take that time out for the Lord, Scripture reading and study, there will usually be distractions and people vying for attention. The day you're trying to fast will be the day that somebody has a birthday or special day, and they want you to come and have lunch or they just happen to bring over all your favorite foods. Then there are all those other distractions like people, children, family, and every noise you can think of when you're really trying to press in and hear from God in prayer. I have used the front seat of my truck as an office, prayer room, music practice room, and worship center on more than one occasion.

Effective ministry stems from staying grounded in God's Word and really hearing from Heaven. Many times, our feelings will deceive us. We're going to have down days, and we're going to get discouraged. We may get swayed by feelings of excitement when certain people come to the Lord, or we see certain responses, but experiences are only a part of who we are even though we praise the Lord for them.

Pentecostal people, and Christians in general, have wonderful experiences, but we cannot base our faith and our foundation on experiences. Our faith and calling must be grounded in the Word of God because we all have those desert experiences when we wonder if God has departed. Staying grounded in the Scriptures will keep us on the right track in our ministries.

Finding a place to study and do research about the community wherein you're speaking can be challenging. Public libraries can be a great place to study on the road, as well as many coffee shops and fast food restaurants where free Internet connectivity is ubiquitous. Don't forget to browse local newspapers if you can, which are often a good way to find out what's happening around the extended area as well. News outlets are a great source of information about the local community and help you write relevant messages wherever you preach.

~ "How many hours does it take to prepare a message?" ~

That really does vary. Some people say you should spend a good 20 hours on a message, and there are times when I have spent that many hours on a good message. There are other times when I've only spent ten hours or less. My progression looks something like this: The Lord begins to deal with me about a certain subject or section of Scripture; then I do some in-depth research on word studies and commentaries; I usually try to bring out some of the original language if there's a word that really sticks out to me; and I try to get an illustration with some personal stories if possible. But it will always vary depending on you, God, and your situation.

There are some messages that only took me about an hour to complete. You may sense a heavy presence of the Holy Spirit, and you just begin writing as fast as you can. You seem to know what God wants to say, and scriptures are just popping into your mind. You basically have the gist of the message in a very short time, but it needs a little more work in order to smooth it out and make it flow well. It really does take between 10 and 20 hours for an in-depth, well-crafted message. It's a lot of work.

I've never been able to completely craft a message in one sitting. I usually put together an outline or rough draft, and then I may feel the leading of the Holy Spirit at some later date to pull that outline back out and complete it. Then I start at the beginning and fill out the message with thoughts, illustrations, Scriptures or short stories. More often than not, the Lord seems to give me tidbits when I need them.

For me, I receive a lot of insights for messages during my worship time—privately or corporately. But we will all have those occasional desert experiences when preparing messages—it just comes with the territory. Don't give up! The enemy usually fights the hardest when great victories are just ahead.

Most evangelists can work on messages anywhere there is Internet connectivity. With the proliferation of free Internet service in almost every town you minister in, your biblical library is only a computer click away. Most hotels also have free Internet and some Recreation Vehicle (RV) parks are now complete with wireless connectivity. I can't tell you how many messages I completed sitting in the front seat of my truck in a hotel parking lot. I was able to work on my message in solitude while letting my family enjoy our hotel room. Just having some quiet time with God—no matter where—was great.

~ Is this what we would call our devotionals? ~

Not really. A devotion time is your set time every day with the Lord for personal edification. As a minister, you also have that study time when you are seeking to go deeper in God and hear His voice for the message He wants you to share. Those special times of fasting, prayer and studying God's word that goes beyond just a devotion of 30 minutes or an hour in the morning when you're praying, reading the Scriptures, etc. But your devotion time counts as my next most important area to safeguard.

GUARD YOUR DEVOTION TIME

You must guard your devotion time to remain strong in your faith and calling. You need to sit and soak in the presence of God, as well as attend other churches when you have an opening. Don't stay home. We all need spiritual nourishment. See if pastors will give you some audio copies of their sermons at the church where you're ministering and listen to them while you're driving on the road. I've had pastor friends who gave me sermons and some of them really spoke a divine word to me—bringing me to tears. We need that. We need to hear the Word of God.

For me, I'm a morning person, so I try to get up early and spend one or two hours praying and reading the word. This is a time that I also ask God for new messages. I don't always succeed at this, but I try my best to have a set schedule for my devotion time. Today, I had to get my son to school at 7 a.m. and last night was a late night. We are trying to complete our ministry newsletter for mailing, and I got about five hours of sleep. So, I'm like, "You know Lord, I love ya, praise Jesus." My devotion was pretty short this morning trying to get ready and get dressed and get out the door. Those short devotion days happen, but they should be the exception rather than the rule.

DR. MARSHALL M. WINDSOR   125

I love my devotion time because this is the time—when I am quiet and alone with the Lord—that I can actually hear the Holy Spirit whisper to me about messages and ministry. Schedules often get busy during the day. So, it's after everybody is in bed or before everybody gets up in the morning when I can really spend some quality time with the Lord. You may have different times that are best for you and different circumstances that necessitate a different approach to your devotion time. Whatever it takes—do it.

⁓ Your devotion time can direct your study time ⁓

Let's say you're having your devotion time and reading through 1st Peter. Suddenly there's one verse that the Holy Spirit really pounds into your spirit, and you're like, "Wow!" The Lord begins to impress the draft of a sermon outline on you, and the message just begins to evolve. Many times, messages are like a good recipe: they just need to stew for a while on the back burner to bring all the flavors and juices together to make it a real quality dish. But sometimes it's a fast meal; like when you go into a fast-food restaurant and "boom!" There it is. The Lord gives you one, two, or three points and a conclusion.

There are also different levels to your messages that you'll find as you grow in your relationship with the Lord. Some messages are really deep, and to me, it's almost like giving birth. It's a process. It's just something that you're struggling to put your arms around, and God is dealing with you in your own spirit. You labor in the Spirit so-to-speak, and I apologize if that sounds a little frivolous. Do I have a right as a man to even say that? Probably not, but it is as though you are laboring. You are toiling, and you don't have a release until you have shared that message.

⁓ What kinds of distractions seem to be most prevalent? ⁓

Sometimes the enemy likes to use poverty, as well as prosperity, to discourage or distract us. Oftentimes in poverty, we will seek the face of God. We get down on our knees in prayer and fasting in order to touch the throne room of Heaven. But it's when we begin to prosper in the ministry that the enemy of our souls causes us to get complacent— leading us to a place where we're self-satisfied. We go through the motions of ministry, but do it in our own strength and ability. That's why we need to have those times of fasting and prayer, going apart to find a place alone with God to really hear from him.

If the Lord chooses to give us financial blessings, perhaps the Lord knows that he can trust us with money. There are people he cannot trust with extra money. These folks may experience poverty and live week to week on what they receive because God knows what they would do if he began to bless them with extra finances. Actually, the whole reason God blesses us is so that we, in turn, will bless other people. He wants us to be a vessel of ministry and blessing to others.

But sometimes—when you have lived with meager finances—you struggle to keep a Godly mindset when money comes your way. Some people begin to have a gripping mentality with money. They feel the need to guard it and protect it and not let anybody in when many times the Lord is testing you to give it away if he tells you to do just that. It is tough, and Satan knows it.

~ Is it normal to feel absolutely nervous with butterflies before you speak? ~

I think that's good. I had a pastor share one Sunday that young people were asking, "how long does it take before you get over your nervousness of preaching?" and he said, "I don't know. You'll have to ask somebody older than me." He is in his 60s, so we all need to realize that this is a feeling we do not need to get over but realize that it's part of our weakness. This actually helps us focus on the Lord who is the ultimate giver of our message. We're just trying to be a vessel for him. That's another reason why our devotion time is so important.

~ Should you be prepared to speak if you visit other churches? ~

When we first started out, if we didn't have a service for that Sunday, we would often visit new churches and introduce ourselves to the pastor. I had some churches, especially in smaller communities, where I went in, sat down, and the pastor came up and asked, "You all are ministers aren't you?" It seemed as though they just knew.

Sometimes they would say, "Why don't you bring the Word tonight?" "Do you want to preach?" I've had that happen. So, make sure you are instantly in season – ha! You usually have about fifteen minutes to get ready. When the Lord does that, it's a bit stressful. I do have some of my messages with me since we're traveling. But, when somebody asks that question, "Do you want to bring the Word?" I say "sure" and then I'm just praying like crazy, "Lord, give me the Word! What do you want me to preach tonight?" The Lord usually prepares you for these impromptu sermons—thankfully.

I usually don't give an actual impromptu sermon, but it may be the Lord will prompt me that there's a message I preached recently that is still fresh in my mind. It's the Lord's gentle nudge telling me that He wants me to preach that message. However, there are places where you just need to be ready, as well as sensitive to the Holy Spirit. I've been in churches where they just walk down the aisle and say, "I feel like you're supposed to bring the Word tonight," and you better start opening your Bible and scribbling notes and whatever else you need.

You may want to carry a message in the back of your Bible for those kinds of situations. But, if the Lord is in the middle of it, He'll help you. You just pray, "Lord you're going to have to fill my mouth tonight. I want you to be glorified," then try to think of some points that you can bring forth. The Lord may bring back an illustration; a little humorous joke or personal illustration and you just really depend on the Lord in those situations. And God's faithful to help you.

Thankfully, God's word is true, and when we are not prepared, we'll be more open to what God wants to say and what God wants to share. So, you might deviate from the message you were thinking about preaching a little more than you normally would. And you really gain confidence. I think the Lord opens these types of doors and exposes us to uncomfortable situations when we're ready for another step. It is a time for God to stretch us so that we depend on God, trusting Him for what's needed in that situation. This is just one more reason why our devotion time is so important because our ministry flows out of our relationship with Jesus Christ.

~ What's the difference between a ministry journal and a spiritual journal? ~

I encourage young evangelists to utilize a spiritual journal because everyone should set some goals or write down things upon which you can reflect during your devotion times. Write down your successes and your failures. It can really be encouraging to read back through your spiritual journal and see where God came through for you again and again. Make notes on personal spiritual breakthroughs or things that the Holy Spirit has spoken to you personally in your time with Him. Note ideas for the ministry or books you want to read, etc. That's why I have a spiritual journal, which is separate from my ministry journal. I talked at length about the ministry journal in Chapter five on scheduling and ministry insights.

Briefly, I use a ministry journal to make notes to myself about every service wherein I minister. I'll write down the pastor's name, pastor's wife and children, directions to the church, what message I preached, and what we sang. I note what happened in the service. Since you see so many different people, it helps you remember the important aspects of a church community when you return. But still, you're relying on the Lord because those people could be gone and things could change. The journal just helps remind me of significant people and circumstances that will help my effectiveness the next time I have an opportunity to minister there.

Ironically, I had a series of services at a church I had ministered in a couple of years before. The pastor was a good friend and when we were visiting after the morning service that first day, he talked about a restaurant where we had eaten, but he couldn't remember the name of it or where it was located. He wanted to take his wife there, but his memory failed him.

I told him I'd look in my journal because I remembered that I had written the name of that restaurant down when looking over my notes from my previous time with him. He was so delighted that I was able to share the name of that restaurant with him. As a matter of fact, we actually had breakfast there one day during that week. Little things like that stand out to church leaders.

But your spiritual journal is a journal for you to be honest with yourself. How are you doing? How's your family doing? How do you feel about the ministry? The Lord is really speaking to me about such and such. Sometimes I use my spiritual journal in my devotion time, what did I read, what did the Lord speak to me today. I don't write in my spiritual journal every day. Maybe a month goes by before I write another entry, but I'll write a page or so of all the things that are going on. Maybe I'll write in it once a week for a while. It's just as the Lord prompts me to write and when I find time to do it.

The greatest aspect of having a spiritual journal is that it encourages you—especially when you have some down times. You can read your journal during your devotion time and see what God has been up to in your life. Some of the things that you were worried about never came to pass, because the Lord came through for you. Your devotion time is where you reflect, rejuvenate yourself spiritually, and refocus for the future. That's because your devotion time is also where you exercise the power of prayer.

GUARD YOUR PRAYER LIFE

David Mohan—a pastor in India whose church seats over 55,000—said prayer is the backbone of a Christian. It really is. Prayer is the lifeline for fresh manna from Heaven, so you must find a regular place of solitude. I encourage evangelists to go to a church when nobody else is there. That's what I try to do when possible. I go to the sanctuary when nobody is there and play the piano or just get alone with God for a while. But, I also pray in a time of devotion for myself. So, you must find that place of solitude at every church.

Most pastors respect your study and devotion time. As a matter of fact, you can ask to utilize certain rooms or the sanctuary at certain times. You can ask them when you're visiting about the church and an upcoming service. Just ask, "Is it okay if I come in on Monday or Tuesday or whenever during the day and pray in the sanctuary?" They may even have prayer times in which they want you to participate. Sometimes, you just have to go for a walk. You have to get by yourself. Do whatever it takes—within reason—for you to hear from God. Many times, prayer and fasting alone are the things that open the doors of opportunity and provide direction.

You don't need to be afraid or feel like you can only hear from God in special places. God can speak to you wherever you are. It doesn't matter if you're in your favorite sanctuary room in your home or whether you're in the bathroom. There are times when I just sit in the front of my truck early in the morning and go through my message. Nobody is around, and I don't have to worry about bothering my family while they are trying to get ready for the service. You must find a place where you can get alone to prepare yourself, your heart, and your spirit for the things that God wants you to do.

GUARD YOUR MINISTRY

You must guard your ministry because you are always working to make it better. We are a reflection and ambassador of Jesus Christ. We shouldn't whine about our problems. It's not about us, it's about the people within a church, country, crusade, or outreach where God has opened a door of ministry. So, we don't' need to whine or complain about everything that's going wrong in our lives. We need to stay focused on the Lord and help the people that God has allowed us to impact at that place of ministry.

We must also stay in touch with new friendships and solidify old ones as we seek to strengthen our ministries. Just calling pastors to let them know you're praying for them and that you care: "I don't want a thing, I just wanted to call and see if you're still laying tile this morning." Perhaps you know pastors who are bi-vocational or juggling more than one additional responsibility. Just work to stay in touch and let them know that you're thinking about them.

Try to honestly be a friend to these folks who are in the trenches of ministry. We would all like to hear, "I just really had you on my heart today and wanted to let you know that I was praying for you." Is there anything special that I can pray with you about?" There may not be anything, but just calling to keep those friendships pays big dividends.

If possible, seek out a good mentor to help you through a lot of the hurdles of life and ministry. Sometimes it really does get discouraging, and it helps to have somebody say, "I've been there. It's going to work out. Get back up and dust yourself off." Having somebody encourage you and keep you accountable is powerful. Then we, in turn, need to have somebody that we can mentor. We need to minister to other people and mentor a Timothy, just like the apostle Paul modeled. There may be someone else starting out in ministry that you could help by sharing some of the things that you've learned. We should all try to help one another.

~ Ministry and planning your schedule ~

Working on our schedule seems like a never-ending job, and I talked extensively about this in Chapter 5. There's that old expression to "plan your work and work your plan" that seems fitting here. Another expression that seems appropriate is the cliché, "if you fail to plan then you plan to fail." It is true that we must make time to plan out when are we going to work on our schedule and be diligent in working on it.

You have an important part to play in scheduling your ministry; filling up empty slots and following up on commitments rests with you.

Then, be aware that mornings are usually best whenever you do begin to call churches and work on your schedule. Mondays and Fridays are usually not good and are often when pastors schedule time off.

You should follow up with the pastors who have graciously opened their doors to you. They didn't have to let you come, but they have opened a door for you to come and if you are the kind of person who never sends a letter and never corresponds or communicates with them, why would they want you to come back? Every evangelist must understand that the burden of building trusted relationships rests with the evangelist.

Long term planning is also a huge part of scheduling; where are you going to be this month? Next summer? Next year? Do you have any mission trips planned? Will you travel with family? You must work to create the most ministry opportunities with the least amount of travel expense. Since church schedules often fill up quickly, a pastor might say, "I'm sorry but we're full this year." If you have done your long-range planning, you can comfortably inquire about any interest in doing something the following year if you already know you're going to be in that area.

Times of planning often happen during my prayer times with the Lord. Even in our personal ministry I sometimes travel alone since my daughter is still in school. When both of our children were in school, we would plan large summer loops of ministry and be on the road for two or three weeks at a time. We still practice that system today. So, we plan out where we are going to go. Are we going to go down south or east or west or north? When we do that, we're going to make a big loop, so we sit down and plan; let's try to get a service around here and maybe one over there on the way back. That way, we are not just driving 12 hours for one service and then driving back. You've got to plan out how you're going to travel.

~ **Ministry and dressing appropriately** ~

You should always look your best. Your clothes don't have to be expensive, but we can buy quality materials to help them last a little bit longer. We can go to thrift stores, look for sales at popular clothing stores, or go to online discount sites. We need to be frugal, especially when we start out in itinerant ministry because every paper clip costs money.

Usually, in evangelistic ministry, it's better for us to dress conservatively. What we wear, our attire, may offend other people or remind others what they can't afford. There are some ministries that dress elegantly. I've mentioned this before, but it merits repeating: You just must realize where you are ministering. Ask the pastor what he or she normally wears on Sunday morning or evening. Ask the Holy Spirit to help your sensitivity in that community so that you're not a hindrance to what God wants to do in any church or outreach setting.

If I'm going to a smaller country church, I'm not going to wear my 5-button suit when most of those people cannot afford those kinds of clothes. Why not wear some slacks, complemented by a sports coat with a shirt, tie, and shoes? Work on just being yourself—being genuine. The Holy Spirit will give you tremendous sensitivity in those different scenarios if you ask him. When you are asked to preach for a conference, then you may feel led to wear your 5-button suit. You will want to look nice and professional—even if that means designer jeans and a T-shirt for more contemporary settings.

When I use the word "conservative," I also think about being flexible. I err on the side of conservative in all my dress. Just like if you use gel on your hair…you gel your hair, but it's not dyed pink. There are different perspectives of what conservative looks like. Conservative in the youth circles is going to be different than conservative in the middle-aged to adult congregations and conservative in children's ministries. I don't want to go so far out that I offend anyone. The apostle Paul said, "To the weak, I became weak, that I might win the weak. I have become all things to all people, that by all means I might save some." (1 Cor. 9:22 NIV).

I want the unchurched to come to know Jesus, and I don't want what I'm wearing to become a stumbling block to them. The clothing styles today are often skin tight, and when a minister wears such clothing, the people focus more on the body of the minister than the Gospel they are trying to preach. Every evangelist should do whatever it takes to keep from being a distraction to the Gospel of Jesus Christ. We should hide behind the cross—not stand in front of it.

For example, if I have a ministry opportunity in a Holiness oriented church I want to make sure that my family is dressed conservatively and that we're not wearing anything tight fitting. Tight clothing would not go over well in that situation, and really seems inappropriate as a representative of Christ in any public venue. But that's just an example of being sensitive to the situation wherein you are ministering.

We must respect their beliefs and who they are just as much as we want other people to respect our perspectives and how we feel. I hear that in young people today, "Why don't you respect who I am and the way I dress and just accept me for who I am?" But it's a double-edged sword. Just because somebody dresses in a suit and tie doesn't mean that they are a square-headed thinking person. We are people too, and we grew up in a different era with a different culture. We still love Jesus. I just dress differently.

Sometimes I want to say, "Don't judge me by what I look like!" But people do. We all judge a "book by its cover." As evangelists begin to minister, they must realize that they don't need to be offensive to younger or older people because they grew up in a different era and have a different perspective—a different mindset. Strive to be like the apostle Paul—so that by all means, we may save some.

Ministry should never be about me and proving my point on whether I'm dressing right or wrong but it's about, "how can I facilitate a smooth connection with that congregation so they'll listen to what God has put on my heart?" I don't want them to turn me off just because of what I'm wearing or not wearing. People are just that way. We're kind of finicky.

GUARD YOUR FINANCES

Guarding our ministry is important, and guarding our finances is another aspect of ministry that is crucial. Although I talked about financial aspects of incorporating in Chapter six, there are a few additional areas of finances that I want to address. Too many people fail to exercise sound fiscal stewardship to include paying their tithes and bills on time. Since the Lord has blessed us with every gift and honorarium, the least we can do is honor his word: "Bring the whole tithe into the storehouse, so that there may be food in my house." (Malachi 3:10 NIV)

~ Has the decline of weeklong meetings hurt evangelists today? ~

I recently talked to an evangelist on the phone who said that a lot of his ministry is weekend ministry or Sunday only. We began to talk about how many evangelists are discouraged because they don't have weeklong meetings anymore. However, I shared that today when you go to a church for a Sunday morning or Sunday night, they will sometimes give you honorariums that are as large as if you would have preached all week. So, it kind of works itself out. Besides, if revival really breaks out, most pastors are open to extending the meeting as the Holy Spirit directs them.

~ But you shouldn't necessarily expect that kind of honorarium - right? ~

No, I don't believe it should be expected. Some pastors will ask you, "What is your budget?" You need to know what it takes to operate your ministry and give a ballpark figure. Some guest speakers say: "Well, I come on a love offering basis only and I pray the church will believe with us that the Lord will provide for our travel expenses above the honorarium to enable us to continue in the ministry." I personally like to stick with the love offering position because you may not always make your budget in one meeting, but the next meeting more than makes up the difference. That's how God often works.

~ Do you have any travel hints to help save money? ~

Travel smart. When you travel with an RV, you can often park in a central location. There are many places where you can spend the night in a parking lot for free. Even when you go to RV parks, try to park someplace central where you don't have to keep moving and maybe drive 20 or 30 miles in different areas to minister for multiple services. If you're traveling extended distances, always try to connect for several services while you're in the area. You can also make a big loop driving over several days when you leave home so that you're not just driving out one time for one service and wasting fuel and time.

Check to see if any evangelist quarters are available at the church or churches where you will be ministering. You might even be able to use an evangelist room in a church for a few days before or after a meeting when you have down days. Some district campgrounds within the Assemblies of God and other fellowships have discounted or free rooms for ministers. Never ask a church for extended hotel accommodations because that is money directly out of their pocket. It's different if they already have an evangelist quarter's setup. That's not really a major cost for them.

For instance, let's say you have a Sunday through Wednesday series of services and the church has evangelist quarters where you will be staying for this revival. You have another meeting that begins the following Saturday night approximately one hundred miles away, and they're going to put you up in a hotel. Prior to coming to the first series of meetings, you could ask the pastor, "Is there any way that I might be able to use that evangelist quarters or rent it until Saturday when my next meeting starts? I'd be glad to pay you a little bit if there is a cost involved." Normally, even if the pastor needed you to pay something, it would cheaper than a hotel. Many older pastors are very open to this and sensitive to the expenses of traveling.

~ Using your cell phone on the road ~

You need to watch your phone usage. Cell phone packages are great and mobile-to-mobile is usually free, but when you're calling other people and churches, phone charges can become expensive depending on your cell phone plan. A church number is not usually a cell phone and will often use your minutes. Some evangelists will use the weekends or late nights to call their family and stay connected. This saves their cell phone minutes so they can talk to pastors and make other business-related phone calls during the daytime.

You also have to watch your family as it grows and determine who gets to have a cell phone. But even with a cell phone, you may have to buy a phone card. Some evangelists use the Internet with computer software to keep an account you can use for video calls and landline calls when you are in a "no cell phone reception" area. You can get inexpensive phone cards at many stores today. You can use those cards when you get to really remote areas in the United States because there are still some places where cell phone reception is unavailable.

Phone cards are also a cheap way to make phone calls when you travel overseas. International roaming fees are huge, so you never want to use your cell phone overseas, but do some research on the cheapest way to use a phone in the country wherein you will minister.

~ Expenses you should prepare for ~

As a minister of the Gospel, you need to make sure you pay your tithes! God blesses those who pay their tithes. If you pay your 10% tithe, then God is going to bless the other 90%. If you don't pay your tithes, Malachi says that the money you have is cursed (Mal. 3:9). So, I'd rather have 90% that is blessed of God than 100% that's cursed of God. Ministers should set the example when it comes to paying our tithes. As a side benefit, it's also a current deduction for your taxes. Your tithes to your church are charitable contributions. Your tithes to your section, district and the national office for credentials are professional dues because if you don't pay them, you won't have credentials.

Keep track of your expenses, your mileage, your hotel, your food, tolls, and tips, everything involved in ministry to include any newsletters mailed and postage used. If your vehicle is used for both personal and ministry, then you have to use percentages. Keep records of your mileage used for ministry and personal use. Mileage notebooks and vehicle logs are available at most office supply stores. You always want to keep your receipts and get a CPA to help answers any questions you may have specific to your ministry or corporation requirements. Be a minister above reproach in your finances.

~ How do you feel about using credit cards? ~

Be a good steward and pay your credit card bills in a timely fashion. Don't live beyond your means. The average credit card debt in America is currently about $7,000 a month. People just leave $7,000 on their credit card and never pay it off. If you have a credit card, you ought to be able to pay it off every month. If you cannot pay it off, then you're living beyond your means. It's easy to keep charging things and enjoy the good life. But you have to pay your bills. When you let credit card debt pile up, then you will often have to pay exorbitant interest on any remaining credit card balance. That is truly not being a good steward. We need to pay our bills, practice good stewardship, and live within our means.

We also need to pay our taxes on time, but not with a credit card. If you're not good at filling out tax forms, then let somebody else help you until you familiarize yourself with the proper accounting forms if you're going to do your own tax work. If you have any legal issues or questions, contact your organization's legal counsel. You should be able to call them anytime. Being a good steward of your finances should be a goal of every evangelist, and with God's help, we can do just that.

GUARD YOUR HEALTH

Make sure you guard your health. We need to exercise and eat right. That's often difficult when you're on the road, but many hotels have small workout rooms where you can exercise. You can also go for walks around the area where you are staying. Utilize hotel facilities if available or gyms that offer day passes nearby. If you're sick, you can't preach, and if you don't preach, then you don't get paid.

~ Fasting and good hygiene ~

We need to fast when the Holy Spirit tells us, but fasting is usually done before meetings. That's because, during your meetings, ministry is very physically, spiritually, and emotionally draining. So, take care of yourself during the meeting. You need to plan on eating at least one meal with the pastor and their family or the appointed person that's going to take care of you for that day. They need to have that time of fellowship too.

You also need to practice good hygiene. You should bathe regularly. Most people don't like to talk about these little issues, but there are many people who never had any teaching in their childhood about hygiene. If you don't bathe regularly—and daily during meetings—or if you don't use soap and shampoo when you bathe, then you will stink and become offensive to others. When that happens, you won't be able to minister to them effectively. In ministry, you will encounter people just like that. They're offensive, and they smell. You'll be praying for them, and the Lord will remind you of what He does not want you to be to other people. He doesn't want you to be offensive.

So, practice good hygiene. Brush your teeth before every service. If you're prone to bad breath, then make sure you brush your tongue when you brush your teeth. All of these things help keep you from being offensive to others. Make sure you shave if needed and use mouthwash before every service. Keep your fingernails trimmed. Utilize breath mints during the altar times. You are leading people to Christ.

One important note: Don't chew gum during your time of ministry. Many people feel it's pretty disrespectful when you're just sitting there smacking gum or chewing gum and trying to tell people about Jesus.

One evangelist I know who was chewing his gum had it fly out of his mouth onto the carpet!

Lastly, make sure you use cologne and perfume sparingly because some people are actually allergic to many fragrances. So, if you're taking a shower and using a deodorant soap or shower gel, then we don't need to put on lots of perfume or cologne.

GUARD YOUR FAMILY

Lastly, you need to make sure that you guard your family. I talk a bit more about traveling with family in Chapter six, but suffice it to say your family is a priority. Your personal relationship with Jesus Christ is obviously your number one priority. But, a close second would be your family and then your ministry. You stand as the priest of your home so regardless of whether you're married or are a single parent you're still the priest of your home. It doesn't matter whether you are male or female; you're still the priest or priestess of your home. As you travel and conduct your ministry, you must remember that the ultimate responsibility for your family's well-being rests with you.

Spending time with your family is critical. There have been too many ministers who tried to win the world and lost their families. Many of these people don't even want to serve the Lord anymore. The greatest legacy that you can leave behind is your family and your children. So, you've got to make time for your family and remember not to steal that time from other people either. Plan family activities and put those activities on your calendar since time is such a crucial thing in our culture today.

Make sure you know all the special dates and activities of your spouse and your children. Things like birthdays, special school functions, dates with your spouse along with daddy-daughter and daddy-son dates or mother-daughter and mother-son dates. Then, don't be afraid to tell people you already have an appointment you cannot get out of so that you can keep your commitments.

~ What about your children and altar times? ~

We should do our best to include our spouses in ministry and make them feel comfortable helping us during the altar time if possible. In our family, sometimes there would be no childcare available in churches where the Lord opened doors of ministry, so Nancy felt responsible for the care of the children while I ministered. The Lord always made a way when a special need for a person of the opposite gender needed prayer. So, focus on taking care of your children and let God worry about special situations during altar time should they arise. If you, or your spouse, feel uncomfortable leaving your child or children with certain folks, just keep them with you.

Make time for your family to eat even when you aren't. Usually when I am getting ready for a service I don't like to eat before I preach. Especially in an evening service since it's right after dinnertime. I just won't eat or will eat very little beforehand. But, I have to make sure my family is taken care of even though I'm not going to eat. Remember that your family depends on you to be sensitive to their needs—as well as the saints to whom you are getting ready to minister. Lastly, love them as much as you can because they grow up way too fast.

PLANNING FOR OVERSEAS MINISTRY

The evangelist in an overseas, or even stateside, missionary context is covered extensively in Chapter ten, but you must plan to employ some system of fundraising to support your mission's projects. Every credentialed Assemblies of God minister can have a short-term missions account and many other organizations have similar support systems. Our account offers a support venue whereby individuals who wanted to help our ministry on a monthly basis can receive non-profit giving credit for their contributions. Evangelists who do not have this organizational option or want more ministry flexibility will need to pursue incorporation if you desire additional support for your ministry. I talk more about incorporation in Chapter six.

Our short-term missions account has been a great vehicle for us to utilize over the years because of our mission's work. If people wanted to support us on a monthly basis, we just told them to contribute to our missions account. When our mission's account accumulates enough funds, we plan a mission trip that allows us to help missionaries already on the field overseas. It has been a great vehicle for our ministry but also kept us from the expense of incorporation early in our ministry. Once you gain a non-profit status, then you can begin taking offerings for the ministry, which strengthens your support base.

Evangelists who incorporate may also have a short-term mission's account so that donors can make contributions as they choose. Many churches may want to give to your missions account because they might receive giving credit through their organization. Individuals would not be as concerned about that, so it's not a big issue for them. Most individuals want to know that their ministry gifts are going to get a tax credit and can deduct any gifts from their taxes.

In the Assemblies of God, any AG minister may have a short-term mission's account, but you can only utilize those monies in that account when you receive an official invitation from an AG missionary on the field of ministry. There is a high level of accountability when you work through organizational channels, so if you just want to pick up and plan your own trips overseas, you will need to incorporate to avoid these types of hurdles.

I personally think accountability is a great thing and has worked for us over the years, but I realize that there are some evangelists who travel to many places where no missionary has been, and this would make it a bit more challenging to gain an "invitation" to travel there. It is always advantageous to work with existing ministries in an area whenever possible, but you would need to check with your own organization on particular areas of concern.

PROMOTION

Pride is the biggest stumbling block of itinerant ministers. Arrogance is arrogance, no matter if you are talking about God or gold. One older male minister said there were three things he always ran from, and those were girls, glory, and gold. I'm sure that ladies could voice something similar: Guys, glory, and gold! When pride begins to take hold of our lives, all the other stumbling blocks seem to rain down upon our lives.

Self-promotion is a somber part of evangelistic ministry. I say somber because it is always a challenge to keep a humble attitude and realize that God alone deserves the glory for any good that comes from your ministry. He is the one who called you. He is the one who protects you. He is the one who draws others to him through your ministry. He is the one who heals and delivers people. In short, God saves the lost—you do not—and you need to always remember that.

~ **Communication and technology** ~

EMAILS

I encourage people not to send spam (unwanted email correspondence) to people. Send invitations to join your email list and make sure you use email software that lets people unsubscribe if they so desire. If someone is your friend, they won't want to offend you. But, if you just add them to your list, then you have put them in a difficult situation—they feel stuck with your emails that they never signed up for and do not want. You have probably lost a friend and gotten some bad publicity at the same time.

There are some venues on the Internet that let you send an invitation to join your email list. When you send out your first email, you can say, "This is an introductory newsletter! If you'd like to receive additional newsletters, please click the link below! Or, if you already get too many emails then don't worry about signing up. I understand the huge amount of information given out today, and you won't be given another newsletter from us unless you personally subscribe to this email listing."

Just send an invitation. Most folks get so many emails already, and they appreciate people who give them a way to bow out or graciously decline an invitation. You need to know your audience and possibly utilize emails with links to other sites. Resources, blog sites, social media, etc. that can help you connect with other ministries and also build your network. Make sure they are people who want to be a part of your network instead of just spamming them and automatically signing them up.

Don't beg for money through you emails or newsletters because it is a real turnoff for most people. It is one thing to present needs tastefully, but to continually ask for money or request that people "sow their seeds of faith" is a real turnoff—especially to me.

NEWSLETTERS

Initially, you're just going to do an annual or a semi-annual, one page, brief newsletter. Be informative, share material that will help pastors and other people who encounter your ministry. Oftentimes people send a newsletter, and it goes right in the trash can. But, if you put a quote or an illustration or something that a pastor could use they just might hold on to that newsletter and look forward to new ones.

That's what we try to do. You can even send your newsletters electronically—just make sure people have requested your newsletter. Most evangelists send emails today because it's an electronic newsletter and it's cost effective to email instead of print and mail. If using email, don't use fraudulent or manipulative means to gain email addresses. That is usually not well received and will tarnish your reputation in the long run. We still send out a regular newsletter except for our friends that are overseas and we'll send them an electronic version.

BLOGS

Blogs are great but don't overdo them since they can steal a lot of time without much impact early on. I've talked to some evangelists who have blog sites, and they've had it for months, and only three people made any comments or visited. It can really take a lot of time away from what God wants you to focus on. Pray about it, test the waters, and see if you get much response.

Most bloggers expect a prompt response to their postings, so don't start something unless you can maintain it. I have found that even national blog sites can fall into disuse over time. It can be frustrating if you spend a lot of money and time to develop something that nobody uses.

To me, that's a real travesty because a minister's heart wants it to be a vehicle of ministry to others. A blog can be a great way to mentor others and allow wiser folks who have been in ministry awhile to speak to the younger generation. But just watch the amount of time you spend on it and monitor effectiveness. That will help you discern when it may be time to end it.

WEBSITES

Websites are another good way to promote your ministry without having to give sales pitches all the time. Keep it relative and short—with pictures. If you are going to have a website, ensure that you keep it updated and full of good content for visitors to see and/or read. You can link to your national and regional offices as well. The Assemblies of God fellowship gives every Assemblies of God credentialed evangelist a free website now. These sites have been shown to help evangelists gain meetings!

The Assemblies of God organization also has an online evangelist directory that helps church leaders find relevant evangelists for their churches. One evangelist told me, "I got another meeting scheduled because of the enhanced online listing." Someone else told me that a pastor called and stated, "I saw your profile and wanted to know if we could get you to come down and share with us."

That directory allows pastors to search by name, address, ministry emphasis, credentialing district, state, city and even dates of ministry. It's a pretty impressive search engine for Assembly of God evangelists. You can find it at http://evangelists.ag.org/directory. Other organizations may have their own directory listings of evangelists so check them out!

All of these venues help get your name and your ministry out in the public eye, but you need to be careful about how you promote yourself. There is a fair amount of promotion that you need to do, and a website will help you. A ministry card or prayer card is also a wonderful investment so that you can remind people to pray for you.

Your ministry grows in steps. You are always working to grow the ministry and make it better. Additionally, you're always trying to be a blessing at every church wherein the Lord opens doors for you to minister.

Most churches today have their own websites. Every evangelist should visit a church's website where they have upcoming services and see what's going on in that community of believers. Get an idea of what the pastor looks like and the pastor's wife; you don't want to offend her by ignoring her the first time you step through the door! Familiarize yourself with the staff if you can and get a feel for what's going on in that church community. Verbalize while you are in prayer, "God how can I be relevant and minister to these people? Show me how." God will reveal the various avenues whereby we can be a blessing.

SOCIAL MEDIA

Currently, social media sites abound and more ministries are adding their presence to the mix of an already crowded landscape. Folks are vying for attention and paying promotional fees to have their names and ministries rise to the top of visibility. They hire social media consultants and staff members who will post incessantly on their behalf. Our lives have become more transparent than ever before through social media and it's all free—if you call losing your privacy free.

That said, every minister must remember that whatever you publish on a social media site will never go away. Even when we delete words, videos or pictures, there is the possibility that our postings may have been captured and copied to various other sites before we can correct errors. Social media is free, and it is a great way to easily update your ministry status and schedule, but one must use caution. Today, there are numerous articles on social media addiction and how it is leading to the decay of social skills and marital problems, so be careful how much time you give to social media. The vast majority of our time should be spent seeking God and His will.

IN SUMMARY

Promotion is an important aspect of the evangelist's ministry that you work on during down times. But, whether it's the online directory or your own website or some other venues: like emails or a listserv you might have, we just need to be professional. You must represent your ministry and the Kingdom of God well through professional, promotional items. Your website may be simple, but is it up to date and relevant? If you're going to have promotional items, then put the effort and resources into them, so they appear professional—because it's representing you. That's going to tell people a lot about you by your promotional materials.

Downtime and promotion are realities of ministry. How you handle these aspects of ministry can make the difference between a full schedule of services and having to leave the field of ministry. You're always working on yourself, strengthening yourself, guarding your time with the Lord, trying to continue to build the ministry and strengthen it. Promotion can be a stumbling stone if we let pride enter into our lives and promotional materials. But with God's help, our downtime and promotional venues will yield a bounty of fruit and glory for the Kingdom of God.

CHAPTER 8

Voices From The Field

No matter what area of ministry you may have studied to prepare for, there are always some situations and issues that you never encountered in a classroom or book on ministry. Thankfully, there will always be those who have gone before us and endured hardships for our benefit. We often call that mentoring today, but many people do not realize that mentoring can come from a variety of sources—even writings from those no longer living.

In the pages ahead, I have gleaned answers to several topics that repeatedly arise in evangelistic ministry and which were posted as questions on an evangelist forum I maintained at one time or another. Numerous evangelists responded to the initial questions, and I tried to put each response in a paragraph format. Although these insights are obviously not all-encompassing, perhaps they will help you grapple with the challenges that may come your way. As an old saying reveals: "We can do more together than we can do by ourselves."

Don't feel as though you need to read this entire section in one sitting. Read it in bits and pieces. Some topics discussed overlap other areas I discuss throughout this book, but I wanted to be as faithful as possible to the contributors in this section and keep their comments complete. You may just want to have it nearby as a reference on areas that you may have questions about. As you read the following pages, allow the Holy Spirit to speak to you about your ministry and how He wants to shape it for the maximum benefit to those for whom He has called you to minister.

BEFORE MINISTRY

Scheduling Meetings

Q: "I have talked to some pastors and evangelists who told me that many churches are scheduling evangelists for only one or two services at a time. Example: Just Sunday AM or PM. Some pastors have stated that they just can't get people to come out to services during the week and they have steered away from weeklong revival services. I would be curious to hear from others as to what they have experienced regarding this issue."

"For every pastor who has told me that they don't schedule revivals (several days) anymore, I have spoken to at least two who tell me they would love to have revivals, but have a hard time finding an evangelist. If my fledgling ministry is illustrative, the first 9 months starting out were slow, and mostly Sundays. I think this was due to calendar considerations (many churches were booked that far in advance, at least) as well as the need to build relationships with pastors.

For the next calendar year, I have conducted or scheduled 20 multi-day meetings ranging from a couple of Sun-Fri revivals to several Fri-Sun formats. The most popular format is Sun-Wed in my experience—more than half of my revivals. From this limited experience, I believe that it is not accurate to say that MOST churches do not host revivals, although this is true of some."

"My personal policy is to go wherever a door is open, regardless of size or financial ability. Therefore, I talk to quite a few pastors who don't have evangelists knocking their doors down (one pastor's exact wording). It seems that often the PERCEPTION is that there is a shortage of legitimate evangelists who are available to them. MY ANALYSIS: I believe that if we don't try to pre-screen churches, the pastors who want to have multiple day meetings outnumber those who ONLY book one-day 'revivals' by at least two to one."

"During my 19 years as a pastor, I rarely scheduled anyone for several days unless I knew him or her and his or her ministry. Usually, if an evangelist contacted me, I would have them for a Sunday night service if they could do that. This would allow me to get acquainted with their ministry, and schedule a revival later if I felt the Lord leading me to do so.

As a full-time evangelist, I preached a lot of Sunday-only meetings for the first year. The few multi-day revivals I had were scheduled with pastors who had a relationship with me. Now, halfway through my second year, more doors are opening for multi-day revivals as a result of those single days. ANALYSIS: Most extended bookings are built on relationships. So, get related! This can be accomplished in ways other than preaching a meeting: Minister's Fellowship meetings, Sectional/District/Gen Council meetings, personal visits, etc."

"I believe that my willingness to be flexible in scheduling has helped me. As a pastor, I ran into some evangelists who would only do a certain format, and as a pastor, I didn't attempt to adapt my plans to fit their format—I asked God to send me another evangelist. As an evangelist, I will minister in a church in any format that I can fit into my calendar. ANALYSIS: Pastors like evangelists who are part of the team, not the guest star. The typical pastor has plenty of *prima donnas* and difficult personalities in his/her church; they don't need to bring someone in from out of town to be a pain in the neck."

"In larger cities, I seem to find more pastors that struggle with getting people out for services and lean more toward Friday through Sunday, Saturday and Sunday, Sunday and Monday, or just a Sunday-only revival. However, they may have felt the same way in Brownsville where God poured out His Spirit in a great revival with evangelist, Steve Hill. When God moves in a huge way as He did then, the plan changes to match whatever God is telling the church leadership and special speaker. Building trusted relationships continues to be the key to open doors of ministry wherever you live."

"I've been on the road now for over 12 years this time and all together for about 17 years; I'm finding that things seem to be changing more and more all the time. Sunday to Wednesday is the usual fare, but this year I've done more weekends than ever before in my ministry."

"Sometimes weekend service offerings are as good as a Sunday to Wednesday series of services. I'm now trying to arrange with some Pastors (with pretty good success), who only want us for the weekend to allow me to stay over and preach the midweek service also. This does two things; it gives me an extra chance to touch their lives and in our case (I travel in a motor home) it provides a parking place for Monday and Tuesday without imposing on them.

To the best of my knowledge, no pastor has ever declined me the opportunity to stay parked at his or her church an extra day or so even if I'm not preaching. However, I do not want to impose on their kindness and have often left a church parking lot to go to an RV park or park at Wal-Mart overnight in order to not impose on them."

"If anyone didn't know it, Wal-Mart currently allows RVs to park free of charge overnight in their parking lots."

Scheduling Into The Future

Q: "I would like some opinions about how far into the future we should schedule meetings. I now have scheduled into spring of next year, not because this year is full for me but because some churches, particularly larger ones, plan their calendars two years and more into the future. Specifically, I want to know if cancellations are much more likely when scheduled in the distant future, or what other issues does that raise? Should we establish some limit how far into the future we should schedule or go into the next decade if a pastor wants to? Any opinions or experiences/war stories are appreciated."

"I would think 2 full years would be plenty, but I know of some children's evangelists that have bookings 3 years out—like your situation that you are not necessarily booked full but that the pastor's (or evangelist's) desired date can only be scheduled that far out. When bookings are farther out, you need to make sure you send postcards / emails at year end or at least 6 months out to ensure you're still on the calendar and that you're looking forward to being with them on _____ (make sure to include the date)."

CANCELLATIONS

Q: How do you handle cancellations?

"When a cancellation comes, it is always a frustrating experience, especially when we are a long way from home. I have no idea what the solution is but would interested in knowing what others do on such occasions."

"Cancellations are never enjoyed, but apparently, they are an occupational hazard. When they come, you might try: Calling the district office and explain that you just had a cancellation and wondered whether they might have any open churches that needed someone to fill the pulpit. You might also ask permission to call the sectional presbyter in the area and see if they might now of some avenues to help.

On another note, make sure you find out why there was a cancellation. Most of the time this is out of your control, but if it is something about you or your ministry (or something that someone told the pastor about you) you need to know about it. It is also important to be understanding (goes without saying) and see whether the pastor will reschedule. Many times, the pastor is embarrassed about canceling and will work to get you in at a later date."

"You can also try calling some evangelist friends that you know have ministered in the area or those that even live in the district where you are ministering. Sometimes they are happy to share a name or two with you, but be willing to give as you have received."

"Thus far I have not had a cancellation that has left me stranded a long way from home, but I think that if I were in that situation, I would try to "pop in" on a service and get acquainted with the pastor. Sometimes you might even be invited to preach, and although the church might not feel any financial obligation in that situation. at least you get a sort of "try out" which at least evolves into a new pastor acquaintance and perhaps eventually a booking."

MAKING CONTACTS THROUGH MAILINGS

Communication is a vital lifeline to itinerant ministers, and most of them have been accumulating their list of church leaders and ministry supporters for years. Promoting your ministry in a respectful way can mean open doors of ministry, but the best way to do that continues to be a matter of sincere prayer. How do you let others know about your ministry in the most efficient way possible? One person started this discussion about district address labels, and I thought some of the following comments might be helpful to share.

Q: "When sending out a flyer or brochure about your ministry do you contact Districts and ask for address labels? Are districts willing to give mailing labels/addresses? Do they charge? Cost? What are some other ways to get mailing addresses without going through websites and looking them up one at a time and then typing them up?"

"When sending out a flyer or brochure, you really need to weigh the effectiveness vs. cost. Most pastors get lots of mailings and districts are not apt to give anyone a mailing list of their ministers. As a licensed minister, you can utilize your church directory that every licensed or ordained minister receives and is often online through your organization. Pick out a certain area that you want to send materials to and draw a circle on the map—then copy the addresses from the church directory. Some organizations allow you to search for churches within a certain mile radius. This is especially helpful when you are in a new part of the country."

"Instead of drawing a circle on a map, I prefer to go online and do a proximity search by zip code. An online directory is much better than a printed one because it is up-to-date. The print one is obsolete by the time you get it. Don't send more mail pieces out than you can follow-up on by phone in a reasonable time."

GETTING TO KNOW PASTORS

When you have an open weekend or service date, you need to take that initiative to drop in and visit churches where you have not been before. When you go, don't expect anything except to possibly introduce yourself and enjoy a good sermon if you join them for a service. Our family recently visited a smaller church and the Lord really moved, and a word of exhortation from the Holy Spirit came forth. It was a powerful time, and I was personally ministered to while we were with them. The pastor was also very gracious and invited me to share a scripture or word (I kept it short).

We also had a great time of prayer at the altars, and afterward, the pastor said that we needed to schedule a revival sometime! I wasn't expecting a thing, and the Lord reminded me that He was the one who had ordered my steps to be there that night. Here are some things that others have shared about visiting and staying in touch with the church leaders with whom they have become friends.

Q: How do you meet new pastors and nurture the relationships you already have?

"When I am in a revival somewhere I spend at least one day just popping in on other local pastors. It helps me to get acquainted with pastors I do not know, and to deepen budding acquaintances. Even if the pastor is not in, leave a card so she/he will know you were there. This is sort of like Brother Marshall's "lunch" idea, except that I can talk to 4-5 pastors in a day—I couldn't afford to take them all to lunch."

"Acknowledge his or her (or their church's) accomplishments: If you see them mentioned in a district newsletter, or somehow on a national level, send the pastor a note of congratulations or note of recognition. Even if the pastor had little or nothing to do with it—like a church event—it is still under his/her oversight, and the pastor will enjoy the recognition. (FYI I have managed to get on the newsletter mailing list for several districts in which I work, where I see these types of acknowledgments. Believe it or not, it is not easy to get on these mailing lists, but it never hurts to ask—and building a relationship with the District Offices is a good thing too.)"

"Birthday cards are nice. (I would hope Christmas cards are automatic). I wouldn't just solicit birthdays, but if I happen to be in a church and note that the pastor's (or family's) birthday or anniversary is mentioned in the bulletin, etc., make a note of it and send a card every year (your computer can remind you). Now, family members might be a little trickier—it's probably not a good idea to send a card to one of them if you don't have the date for them all."

"When you hear of a death or serious illness in the pastor's family, a note of condolence or get well wishes—along with your prayers, of course."

"Find occasions to stay in touch when you're not trying to book a service."

"I have been told that personally written cards and notes cause people to stop and appreciate your thoughts and wishes far more than all the typed letters they get today. Be different—be a "Purple Cow." (A great book by the way—although secular, it stirs the creative juices)."

Sunday Night Services

Q: How has the decreasing number of churches having Sunday night services affected other evangelists? How is it affecting their scheduling of revivals or revivals in general?

"Churches which do not normally have evening services that DO want to schedule a revival, usually do so. In my 27 months of full-time evangelistic ministry I have only encountered that situation twice, and in both of those the church simply had a revival service on Sunday night and the people seemed excited about this 'new and different' service. In fact, both of those churches had Sunday evening prayer meetings for a month leading up to the revival. On the other hand, churches, which do NOT want to schedule a revival, simply won't, and the Sunday night schedule has nothing to do with it. Sometimes I have a morning service in one of these churches and begin a revival in another church that night."

"I am still doing a lot of 'get acquainted' services in churches where I am not known. If a church only has morning services, that opens a door for me to call another church in the area and offer to come for the evening service, and often pastors take me up on this as a way to introduce my ministry to their church. Overall, it seems to be a positive impact on my ministry."

DURING MINISTRY

Ministry Introductions

Q: How much time should you limit yourself to for introducing your ministry?

"It really depends on what service it is. On Sunday morning, I try to get to the ministry ASAP since time is so critical. Sunday evening I take time to explain a bit about our ministry, our needs and the costs of our CDs and tapes, maybe as much as 15 min or so. Hopefully, the other nights are no more than 5—10 minutes tops, just enough to greet the people and express appreciation for the offering. I'd sure be interested to know how that compares with others. I do not say what I do is right; it's just what I do. I attended a service one night of a nationally known evangelist and he never so much as said hello. He just walked to the pulpit and said open your Bibles. I've also been in a service with another popular evangelist who told jokes for 30 minutes or so before he got to the message. It seems that both of these evangelists were a bit extreme."

"I tend to lean more towards the 5-10 minutes unless I'm showing a PowerPoint or something about a mission trip—almost always in an evening service when we're in a place for more than one service. I don't think I would dwell on the product table too much...let the pastor talk about that if possible."

"Personally, I never mention our product table. I always leave that up to the host church, if they want to mention it. I have been in services where an evangelist took a long time just going through what they had on a product table. I am not sure that it gives a good impression and I don't want to look like a peddler for the service. I have found that when our product table has been in a visible location, people always tend to find it."

"If we are in a church for one service, I always take a few minutes to introduce who we are, etc. If we are in extended meetings, I normally take the first service to introduce ourselves, then on the other services I don't linger on it much. Since the majority of our meetings are Kid's Crusades, I normally make our formal introductions in a Sunday morning service."

"I would have to agree with you, 5-10 minutes maximum. I am just beginning the ministry as an evangelist, so I do not have a lot to say from that perspective. But as a former Senior Pastor, I found that my people in the congregation and I wanted to hear about the evangelist's ministry. But, you must remember that the people came there to hear the word preached and be ministered to in some way. People's attention spans are only so long. I believe the evangelist should use most of his speaking time to preach the Word and minister. That's why probably five minutes is long enough for an introduction to ministry."

"If the pastor is a friend of yours let them introduce you to his or her congregation. That will show the people that the pastor has put his or her stamp of approval upon your ministry, and then the people are more willing to receive from you what God has for them."

Sermon Length

Q: What length of sermon is most effective in the morning service? And in the evening service?

"I run about 30 minutes tops, maybe 40 for the morning service."

"I try to finish by 12:00 p.m. in the morning service. In the evening service, my wife gives me a little secret signal when I've gone 40 minutes, and I try to wind down from there. I frequently go one hour. I do not say that's right; it's just what I do."

"It seems like I run about 30-45 minutes as well, but it does depend on how the congregation is responding as well as the Holy Spirit. I strive to shorten my messages in the morning as I am trying to connect with the congregation, introduce my family, ministry, etc. I always want to make time for folks to come to the altar...then it's in the Lord's hands."

"Morning: Beyond 30 minutes seems to be wasteful time that can be used for altar time. Most have a tendency to repeat, which is only productive in rare cases. Evening: Same 30 minutes. 80% of the population has an attention span of less than 30 minutes."

"Yep...it definitely depends on the part of the country you're in and the audience you're speaking to. Seeker sensitive folks tend to prefer shorter messages and old-time Pentecost folks seem to like longer, just better pray and see how long the pastor normally preaches. ☺"

Spouse Appreciation

Q: How do you show appreciation for your spouse during your times of ministry?

"Before I preach I always acknowledge my wife and let the audiences know how much I love and appreciate what she does for me. I could not do it without her."

"I like to make it known in the very first service, whether she is with me or not, that she is my best friend and that our relationship is sound and we are very much in love. I want her to know it, and I want the congregation to know our 41-year marriage is happy and totally satisfying. I believe it makes her feel special and causes the congregation to have more confidence in us. I also want her by my side in the prayer lines. Again, I want her, and the congregation to know she is vitally important to what I do."

"Usually in one of the first services I introduce the family (whether they are present or not), and when I get to my wife I tell the congregation that I truly appreciate a godly wife who prays for all three of her children... me included. Since we only have two children, this helps break any existing tensions and helps in connecting with a new group of people, all the while publicly admitting that my wife is very special to me."

"When submitting my bio for churches to use for PR purposes and for them to introduce me from the pulpit, I list all the ministries I am involved in and my credentials, and then as my last line I say: 'But my most important ministry is my husband of 20 years and our 19-year-old son.'"

HELPING PEOPLE MOVE TO THE ALTAR

I feel that one of the most loathsome acts of any itinerant minister is altar manipulation. I have seen it done in a number of settings and it truly disturbs me every time I witness this gross abuse of power. It is one thing to extend a passionate invitation to "get your heart right with God" or "make a decision for Christ," but it is another to manipulate people's emotions and passion for personal results or photo opportunities. I love the way Billy Graham would always extend the invitation for salvation and then begin to pray silently. So, I asked how other itinerant ministers were led of the Holy Spirit to extend their invitations. Perhaps some of these insights will be helpful to you as well.

Q: Is there anything that helps get folks moving toward the altar when you know God has spoken to your heart about a certain thing, but no one seems to want to respond?

"When I have an altar call I will say: 'EVERYONE who needs healing come forward' instead of saying; 'If there is ANYONE who needs healing come forward.' No one likes to be the only one, and this seems to help people respond to the altar call because there is a possibility that others will respond, too."

"We try to put people at ease with their need to respond. For example, if you are doing a healing service, most people who need some form of healing will remain spectators. Pride makes people guarded; most people don't want to feel like they are abnormally needy. If you put people at ease with their need, that they are not the only strange person who needs to respond, most will then respond. Instead of asking those who need a healing to respond, we ask: "Is there anyone in the room in absolute perfect physical health with no deficit whatsoever?" The people usually laugh, and then we share how everyone can ask God for healing for their need—whether it is big or small. You can feel the whole room relax."

"I realize that once people are at the altar, the Holy Spirit can do whatever He pleases, but I believe it puts people at ease to respond if they understand exactly what you are calling them forward for. Again, I know once we get there, God can do whatever He wants to, but when I pray for people to receive the Baptism with the Holy Spirit, I like to help them understand the pattern we will be following, i.e. Acts 19:6. If we are going to pray for the sick, I want them to know how we will go about it, laying on of hands, anointing with oil, etc. I often will ask people to stand in a particular area so we will know just how we are to minister to them. I want it to be clear that I give plenty of room for the Spirit to do whatever He wants to. However, if we do not get them to the altar, it is difficult to minister anything to them."

"I also frequently will make it a team effort, i.e. 'take someone by the hand and walk to this place of prayer together.' I'm a firm believer if we can get them to the altar the Holy Spirit will do for them what they need."

HOME REMEDIES FOR A STRAINED VOICE

Undoubtedly, one of the most important resources a minister has is his or her voice. When you cannot speak, you cannot function as the Lord intended so taking care of your voice is crucial. You may hear ministers talk about how they had to really "plow" during a message, letting someone else know that the spiritual oppression or disconnect with the congregation was hard to break through. Sometimes, when this happens, it is easy to overexert your vocal chords and strain them. Some evangelists refer to this phenomenon as "stripping your gears." I have also found that poor sound systems, wherein it is difficult to hear yourself, can lead to unnecessarily raised voice levels to compensate for low volume in monitors or an unqualified sound person.

Q: What remedies seem to work best for you when you find you have strained your voice and you are having difficulty speaking?

"I have tried lemon juice in the past. It seems to help. I try to avoid straining my voice if possible. Keeping the microphone adjusted for my voice helps a lot."

"In my case, I suffer more from laryngitis due to sinus drainage, and of course when your vocal cords are inflamed because of that your voice can be damaged by almost any use. Keeping your throat lubricated/ hydrated is the best thing you can do (after controlling the drainage as best you can), and my favorite product for that is Hall's cough drops, which open up breathing passages while lubricating my throat. In one revival where I was struggling with my voice, the pastor suggested orange juice, said it gives energy and helps strengthen your voice. He even provided bottles of OJ in the pulpit for me."

"Here are some 'home remedies' that seem to work, albeit most people agree that keeping the water close so you can keep your vocal cords lubricated is a must and after over exerting, rest is the best bet. But when you can't:

- Some Ibuprofen at least 1/2 hour before going to bed seems to help me when I've over exerted myself and the vocal cords are inflamed.
- During revivals, hot tea (with lemon if possible) is a lot better on your voice than coffee.
- Some people like to gargle with very hot salt water.
- Spicy V-8 juice with a little cayenne pepper cuts the phlegm and helps soothe the throat—honest (I'm told—haven't tried this one yet).
- A dentist told me that 1-tablespoon of apple cider vinegar (the dark kind) and 1 tablespoon of honey in very hot water does wonders to neutralize the acid around your vocal cords (and stomach) and allows quicker healing. Just sip the mixture and as your throat pickles it actually helps—go figure—it does smell a little like dirty socks, though."

"I have a brother who is an ear, nose, and throat doctor. For speaking, he always suggests at least water. Lemon water helps as well."

"Cough drops always seemed to help as long as you do not move them around in your mouth too much and click them against your teeth, the wireless microphone will always pick up that sound and everyone will know what you have in your mouth. I have found that having an unwrapped cough drop in your pocket is easy to grab."

"Have the microphone turned up more than usual, so you do not strain your voice any more than you have to."

"If you are just drinking water, make sure that you have two glasses under the pulpit or nearby, because with your voice already strained you may go through the first glass quickly."

"I always wondered about the cough drops or breath mints in the pocket thing. I was always afraid I'd wind up with a lint ball before it was all said and done! I was told some people sew a plastic lining in their pocket, but I was wondering how that gets by the dry cleaners?"

"I like to drink hot ginger root tea, made with fresh ginger root. This soothes the throat. Simply get a large piece of fresh ginger root from your local grocery store. Cut off a big chunk, shave the skin off and then cut into several pieces and place in a mug. Add some hot water and let it steep for a while, stir and sip. Repeat as often as you like."

"While speaking—have some water handy and instead of using Halls cough drops I like to use Fisherman's Friend lozenges. Now these things are pretty strong, so I'll usually snap a few of them in half, and put in my pocket and pop them in my mouth every so often. I find they work better than the Halls."

"Never heard about the ginger root tea, but it sounds like a pretty good concoction to try (better than snake oil no doubt<G>)."

"On those Fisherman's Friend cough drops—those of you who have never had one watch out:)—they are definitely strong. When I had a cold one time with a cough I got some of those and after one cough drop my cough almost vanished—it was afraid I was going to take another one of those Fisherman's Friend cough drops<G>. Sounds like a good idea to snap them in half."

PRODUCT TABLES

Q: How much time should you spend talking about your product table? Have you ever asked the pastor to introduce your product table?

"The obvious answer is *as little as possible*. I spend almost no time talking about my table, figuring that most people are smart enough to figure out what it is as they walk by. Occasionally, I will introduce a song with something like, "This is on our new CD out on the table in the foyer." On a few occasions, mostly when I am speaking for a youth event I will give away a T-shirt for answering a simple question about last night's message, etc., which draws attention to the table without overt salesmanship."

"Speaking from my 19 years of pastoral ministry, one of the things I liked LEAST about guest ministers was for them to take valuable pulpit time to promote their products. I believe that if one surveyed pastors, this would be one of the top two or three gripes about evangelists. As to the second part of this question, I have never asked a pastor to talk about my table. But, on a few occasions pastors have taken it upon themselves to do so when they realize that I am not going to—I believe in appreciation of my not wasting pulpit time doing it myself."

"I seldom say anything about my product table on Sunday morning. Sometimes I will simply mention that the message is being recorded on cassette and CD and will be available at our table immediately after the service. On Sunday night, I go into more detail about prices and what is and will be available. On the evening before the closing night, I will mention it, asking people to sign up for the set so we will have some idea of how many sets to prepare. Perhaps I spend too much time on it, but that is my procedure. After hearing at the Evangelists Conference that about 25% of responding Pastors say that time spent mentioning the table is a problem, I plan to spend some more time consulting with each Pastor about how much time I should allow for this."

"I only offer two items on the table that are not my own products. It is my firm belief that I have more to offer a congregation in my messages than I can give to them in just the few services I am with them. Therefore, any message I can leave behind with them will add to their spiritual growth as well as provide some profit with which I can purchase diesel to get my coach the next meeting. I also frequently make mention of the fact that if anyone actually cannot afford the product, I will be more than happy to give them what they want for free. I do not ask Pastors to mention the table but always appreciate it when they do."

Q: Is it wise for a new Evangelist to even be concerned about offering products or not? In my case, I would have little to offer on a table at this point, but will certainly have more in the future. The next question is how much of each item do you take to a meeting? How do you determine stock levels?

"There are many folks who don't have products tables due to the same issues you have. It does cost a bit to start producing product and that is another whole world to investigate. Just start where you are with a goal of having a table in 6 months, a year, etc. When you are able to get a first class recording of a message keep it in a safe place until you can get a few more."

"On the money, I have heard more than one person state that they try to at least double their money. If something cost them $5 they ask $10, etc. Some evangelists are much more generous and really try to cut costs so they can offer something affordable to everyone. You can also get a feel for what others are doing—are their CDs $5 or $7, or something else. What packages or specials do they promote? Ask pastors as you minister how they feel about product tables and what they think is tasteful. A pastor's perspective is a pretty good thing to keep in mind."

A word of caution...

Just ask the Lord to guide you in your products so that you are maintaining a first-class ministry with quality materials that will be a blessing. Make sure you have the pastor's blessing to set up a table whenever you do have a product table. In a national survey by the Assemblies of God National Evangelists Office, pastors stated that they did not like it when evangelists seemed more concerned with getting to their product tables after the service than staying around the altars and praying for people. A danger is that there can be a tendency to focus more on the product table than the pulpit that God has called us to fill. It's still a God thing regardless of what we do.

"To respond to one of your questions, I keep two of each identical item on the table, with everything I own in tubs out of sight where I can replenish every day. Too much stuff on the tables makes it look like the blue-light table at K-Mart. As to where to start as a new evangelist, I recommend recording and offering CDs or DVDs of the services. A person who is particularly blessed, healed, called to ministry, etc. in a service may cherish a recording of that particular service. When placed alongside pre-recorded CD albums of sermon series, etc., the contemporaneous recordings will outsell pre-recorded ones by about 5 to 1 because of specific meaning a particular service will have for a person."

"Equipment to record and duplicate CDs or DVDs is not tremendously expensive—I mined eBay for some of mine—and will probably be recouped in 2-3 months of services at most. As to what to charge, observing what churches sell their recordings for, etc. is good advice, but I would encourage you to consider offering them on an offering basis. Often the net proceeds are about the same as if you put a price on them, and it allows the truly poor to still be blessed even if they only have a dollar or two to give. It also makes a statement that the ministry of your product table is more important than the income from it."

"I see varying opinions and convictions about the product table. That's great. Go with what God leads you to do."

"For my two cents, we carry 3 basic types of items: our worship CDs, our books and our teaching CDs. We have found that a disciplined two-minute announcement in each service, which highlights two or three products, works very well. We highlight different products in each of the different sessions. Pastors consistently remark privately how much they appreciate the brevity, but also how much they appreciate the materials getting in the hands of the people."

"Over many years, we have seen and tried several "deals," but none have been as well received as a 'buy 2 get the 3rd for free' deal. It just seems to work best for us."

"Our rule of thumb for items on the table is that we must be personally convicted that they are life changing. Consequently, I have many sermons that I can't sell!"

"We made the commitment in our first year on the road to give each pastor one-of-every item on our table—each week. This is not only a great way of saying thanks, but also a great way to encourage and be a long-term blessing to them. We also give a few items to each staff pastor. God has really blessed this."

"As for us, we do t-shirts and offer our service CDs on a love-offering basis. And we do very little promotion from the pulpit. Most pastors like it that way and will promote our table for us when they see we are not trying to be a moneychanger. I tried the "set price" thing, and it bombed quickly; I also give a set of CDs to the pastor, and if he has kids, Pam and I give the PK's (preacher's kids) a t-shirt apiece. When you bless the pastor and his family, it goes a long way to building a lasting relationship."

"As per pricing products, it is my understanding that if the money goes through your non-profit you really need to offer products as a suggested donation. If you are set up with a resale license (start in your home state) then you can sell the items for a set fee and the money would not run through your non-profit."

"Great point. I bounced this off our legal counsel, Richard Hammar, and here is what he had to say:

Like Isaac Newton said about computing the orbit of the Moon, 'the complexity of it makes my head hurt.' So, it is with the issue you have raised. Does an evangelist incorporated in State X, who conducts services in State Y (and perhaps several other states) must collect sales tax on items he sells?

I would direct you to Chapter 12 in my annual tax guide for a brief discussion of sales taxes, along with a table at the end of the chapter that quotes the main provisions of the sales tax laws of all 50 states.

What makes your questions uniquely complex is the multistate nature of the matter.

I did talk with a local CPA, and he said that people should check out what each state requires. Some states don't require anything if you are only there for a limited amount of time, while others say you must register no matter what. Whether you are incorporated or not is a consideration as well.

The donation issue is a valid venue and one that deserves more attention—just remember that any receipts must deduct the product value from any donation if tax receipts are desired."

Dealing With The Television

Q: How do you deal with the cable TV in your motel room? Do you watch it / keep it off / only watch it with family?

"Normally, I am always with my wife and daughter as we travel as a family. We are very selective in what we view. Most motels have a channel listing of what they offer, and we usually take a look at that. We usually stick to the Family channel, Hallmark channel and as of lately on occasion, Animal Planet, for our five-year-old. She loves animals! If I were on my own; however, I might prefer just to leave the TV off. At our home, we don't have cable and only pick up about three channels. Even on the non-cable channels, we have discovered that on several occasions they do not rate our time due to the nature of the content. It is a real shame what they will allow to air on regular TV. DVDs and videos are much better because we can judge what we are viewing."

"My wife is always with me when we travel because of a condition called, (fibromyalgia) which is a disorder that causes me a lot of muscle pain. So, she basically takes care of me. So being on my own is not a problem. But we have found that usually after ten o'clock stations such as Showtime, HBO, and other movie channels have terrible pornographic garbage on them. And even when flipping through the channels, you can come across a slight glimpse of them, which that image can stick in your brain for quite a while; especially a man's brain. And as a man, I do not want to put garbage in there.

So generally, we do not watch television in hotel rooms after ten o'clock. If we happen to watch something after 10 p.m., it is usually the weather, news or an old movie. We try to look in the guide and find all the movie channels there are and make sure to skip over them."

"When we were youth pastors and then pastors of a small church, we would take teenagers to youth conventions. At those, you are normally put up in a hotel. Then you have the duty of monitoring what the teenagers watch. Especially the boys, but the girls can get into a lot of garbage as well; which neither boys nor girls need right after a great service where God has touched their lives.

In this situation, if there is one available, a KOA or other such campground would work great. The girls would get one cabin, and the boys would get another, and there is no television. Instead of television you can sit around a campfire and discuss what God has done in their lives. Plus, a KOA is usually cheaper than a hotel room and a lot more fun. For you and the teenagers."

"The KOA cabins are a good alternative for the evangelist who's on the road. Of course, if you have a motorhome to travel and live in, (like we hope to have someday) cable TV is not a problem."

"That is a great idea on the KOA or any other place where you can get outside (if it's not 30 below zero<G>!). We love the outdoors and I find that not watching TV doesn't hurt me too much—ha. We also try to get out and see the local sites of interest if possible to help show our children that itinerant ministry can be fun in and out of the church setting."

"If I'm traveling without my family, I try to spend an extra portion of time with the Lord and work on new messages, etc. I usually get the news updates when I'm online checking email or doing other work.

When the family is with me we often just end up watching the food channel (of all things!). There does seem to be a lot of garbage out there, and that is one thing I don't need when trying to hear the voice of God."

OTHER AREAS OF INTERESTS

District Council Booths

"I ENCOURAGE EVERYONE TO TRY AND MAKE IT TO HIS OR HER DISTRICT COUNCILS, SECTIONALS, AND ANY OTHER MINISTERIAL MEETINGS." -MW

In most organizations, sectional, regional or district conferences occur on a regular basis. The larger conferences and conventions, like district or regional meetings, usually happen once a year, while an organization's main convention may be a biennial event. As itinerant ministers, visibility is often a key to making new friends or efficiently sharing the latest news of your ministry or missions' endeavors. The following question talked about district events and how available vendor booths were to itinerant ministers.

Q: Has anyone had much luck in setting up an evangelist booth at his or her local district council conference? Did you contact the district and ask for permission or do they contact you? Is there usually a charge for this? Letters and e-mails do not seem to be very effective in "getting my name and ministry" out there. I was considering having a table at my local district council conference (pictures, pens, candy, info) but did not know how effective it might be? Thoughts? Comments? Suggestions?

"I encourage EVERYONE to try and make it to his or her district councils, sectionals, and any other ministerial meetings. Not necessarily for bookings, although that's nice; but, evangelists always know a few openings they have in their head anyway. Pastors expect an ambush so surprise them by just working on friendships, and you'd be surprised how often that turns into ministry opportunities! Most importantly, being present at major events helps pastors realize that they have evangelists in their midst and it also helps them know who their evangelists are—and getting to hear some great messages is just a bonus. OK enough about that!"

"Districts differ on availability and pricing of booth spaces. You will have to call your organization's district or regional office(s) to inquire on whether you can have a booth, how much, dates, etc. Some districts are free—most are not. Prices range from about $50 to $500 (most are cheaper) depending on the size of the district. If you talk to the district leadership they might allow you to have a discounted price—sometimes district dues-paying folks get discounts."

"On the booth, here is what I've found works for me (anyone else feel free to chime in). Candy is okay, but chocolate stops them every time—Hershey kisses are relatively cheap, and people love them. Don't put them all out at once, but have some in a container (bowl, basket) and about a dozen on the front edge of the table so people can "snatch" them without feeling obligated to stop.

Don't go to the expense of pens, mugs, and shirts—unless you have the money to spare. Anything with your ministry name is a great tool— if you have the finances. BUT, the main items you need to have if you are going to incorporate a booth are a quality brochure and a free DVD or CD. It would be nice if you had some nice ministry cards and any "tasteful" product that you might have. I also have one friend who puts a ministry label on a small packet of Kleenexes since most folks enjoy grabbing a free packet to put in their purse or coat pocket."

"The main thing is not to attack people when they come to your table but just be cordial and "let them shop!" If they have questions be close enough to ask but far enough away to not bother them. It can also be beneficial if you "leave" for periods of time—that gets rid of the intimidation factor. DON'T sit down—that's almost saying, "I don't care if you're here." Stand in front of your table, if very crowded, but to the side, so people can easily get to the front of your table. Greet everyone and be as nice as you want him or her to be to you. A lot of folks will still avoid you like the plague, but God will have some divine appointments for you when you prayerfully approach this venue as striving to glorify His name."

"I am planning on having a booth at a neighboring District's Council and appreciate your suggestions. My question is would a drawing be worthwhile? I have in mind probably a golf shirt—I do my own screen printing and have a stock of these available at reasonable cost, BUT, would that actually cause more traffic at the table, and/or allow more opportunity for conversation, etc.? I'd appreciate any insight the peeps (people) have to offer."

"Whenever I have done a drawing it has helped bring some additional attention to the booth. Of course, if you wanted to offer a new electronic gadget, that might bring quite a bit of traffic<G>. I have found that most people don't want whoever staffs the table/booth to be like a vulture... it drives them away. I usually try to do a variation of being present and absent to let anyone feeling threatened an opportunity to stop by and sign up before I get back. The more councils/booths you participate in, the more you get a feel for what works and what doesn't."

Guarded Time

Q: How do you guard the time needed for ministry preparation?

1 Peter 5:8 tells us to: "Be sober-minded; be watchful. Your adversary the devil prowls around like a roaring lion, seeking someone to devour." One of the things an itinerant minister—and all ministers for that matter—must do is guard your time of ministry preparation. That includes your times of prayer, sermon preparation and even your time following your ministry. The enemy of your soul is constantly trying to distract you with some very worthwhile and even important things so that you do not have adequate time to prepare for ministry. With that said, here are a few insights concerning your time that may be helpful to you.

"I am a morning person, and I've found that keeping the best part of my day for Scripture and prayer always helps the rest of my day. When traveling, sometimes I have to go sit in the front seat of our truck for my quiet time. Traveling with a family can challenge your opportunities for some solitude with the Lord. But, I have found that God is not so much interested in the place of your preparation as the person and passion for His perfect will."

"I agree! If you stay in the Word, it keeps you focused on prayer, and sensitive to the issues that God is concerned about, which are souls, and the redemption of the lost."

"For these forty years, I have endeavored to give Jesus about three hours of prayer each ministering day. My best time to function is in the morning. That may be a hindrance since the evangelist is called to do his best work in the evening. However, two hours of prayer during a prayer walk each morning sets the tone to be sensitive to the Spirit of Jesus. The exercise is good for the body. "Bodily exercise profits a little." Then, I have found it well to spend the last hour before the service praying in the sanctuary. In order to "keep in shape" spiritually, I endeavor to pray one hour each on non-ministry days."

Ministry Promotion

Some people believe an evangelist should let God completely open doors for him or her. Others say that you must believe that your ministry belongs behind every pulpit in the world and it needs to be promoted with gusto—then there is everything in between.

Q: How do you promote a new ministry?

I'm sure there are as many opinions here as there are evangelists. I always encourage evangelists to start where they are (i.e. spending money on posters, letterhead, fancy cards, etc. may not be the best use of your (or your spouse's) funds early on. Building a network of relationships is the number one key to longevity in evangelistic ministry.

You do that by going to sectional meetings, women's functions (if your ministry impacts them), district functions, calling, writing notes, etc. Send annual letters, newsletters (get a nice printer and do them yourself), and other means to maintain existing relationships—they are your best publicity!

When you get the money (or a church wants to help you) get some nice quality, professional, cards. You can do a lot with those and even make your own ministry posters by getting card stock at Wal-Mart and gluing your "professional" card (did I say professional?) with some verbiage to the card stock (you can utilize different colors to attract attention). Posters are nice, but a lot of churches don't even put them up. Missionaries use the card stock and "professional" card method so why can't evangelists?

"I say to seek God for a plan. I use a system of making acquaintance with pastors which I feel came to me from God in my time of prayer as He was leading me into evangelistic ministry. I will happily share the details of my system with anyone who wants to know, but that might be like Gideon telling Army Generals how to attack 135,000 Midianites with 300 men—it probably won't get the same results for you because it's not God's plan for YOU. But I believe that if He has specifically called you into this type of ministry, then He DOES have a plan for providing a platform from which you can accomplish your calling."

Online Access

In a day when almost every food chain has wireless (Wi-Fi) connections to the Internet, the world has definitely gotten smaller. However, there are many times when itinerant ministers are in remote areas where an Internet connection is a priceless commodity! As technology evolves, we may see many changes to the different responses below, but currently, these are all still viable options when you need to find telephone service and an Internet Service Provider (ISP).

Q: How are some of you accessing your ISP? What services are best for us who travel? I have been using my cell phone for access but this summer we have been in the far NE, and this method just isn't available in this area. I travel in a motor home and connect the coach to the church's phone lines (with consent of course) when I can. How are others doing it?

"We utilize a laptop, which has wireless capabilities. We have discovered that a lot of towns have wireless Internet connection points that are easy to access. But, I do know that in some towns, it is difficult to access the Internet. In those cases, I will usually visit the public library to check mail, but for the most part, we can usually find access over wireless."

"Public libraries are good, as well as some coffee houses (i.e. Panera, Starbucks, etc.), and many fast food restaurants. Some churches even have high-speed access to the Internet. I found many of the RV parks (in the NE) have Internet, but you do have to share, and it's dial-up in some places. I have used phone cards when in really remote areas, which can be set up in communication software packages. I also have friends that have cell phone service providers that provide cards for laptops so that you can call up and download email, etc. at somewhat high speed. I have also found that the number of free Wi-Fi hotspots is growing and this website can help you locate one near you http://www.wififreespot.com."

"My cell phone carrier is Verizon, and I utilize it to access my ISP. Verizon sells a home office kit (I believe that is what it is called) that allows you to go online with the cell phone. My plan has free nights and weekends, so I can use it then with no worry about minutes used. It is slow, however, but far better than nothing. Some Verizon areas (I'm not sure it is available in all Verizon areas) have access that they call "near high speed."

When I am not in a Verizon area, the service still works in their "extended area" at least in most places. I've been in Northern Maine the last several months, and it does not work here at all. However, when you are an area that it works in it is very handy (running down the road with my laptop works nicely as has been mentioned)."

"I did obtain a Verizon laptop card about 4 months ago. They just added it as another line to my existing account (it has its own phone number). It works at "near DSL" speed in most areas, and at 14.4 kilobytes per second (yes, blindingly slow) in many remote areas. Basically, anywhere Verizon service is available I can get on the Internet one way or another. It is great to be able to check email, MapQuest directions, etc. while riding down the road. The downside is that it is subject to sudden interruption (dropped call) just as a cell phone is, but it doesn't happen very often for me."

DIVINE PROVISION TESTIMONY

I received this wonderful testimony from a fellow evangelist, and it reminded me of all the times I preached on faith, but always struggled when I was in the place where I needed faith. By the way, that's the interesting thing about miracles—most people do not want to be in the place where they need a miracle! Everyone loves to see miracles, and I know that God still performs the miraculous even today, but being in the place where you need a miracle is an altogether different story. So, listen to my friend, Tim, as he shares what God did for him; and be encouraged that the God of the Bible still has a miracle for you if you need it.

July and August found me 900 miles from home with four out of seven weeks that I would be in this area completely open for one reason or another. When I arrived to preach the first revival I had virtually no money, even for gas to get to the next meeting. The church where I ministered first is very small and struggling financially. They did their best, but the offering barely covered the gas to get here—and almost half of that came from the pastor himself. Then, when I was at the end of my rope with nowhere to turn and no money to get to my next meeting nor money to get back home—God kicked in.

Over the next three weeks, ALMOST EVERY DAY, money arrived from somewhere. Several times my wife called, saying, "Tim, we got a check in the mail today." After a few days of that, it was, "Tim, we got ANOTHER check in the mail today." Some of it was payment for odd jobs I had done six to eight weeks before, and they finally got around to paying me. On a couple of *occasions friends just handed me money. One old friend, a retired evangelist that I worked with for one summer as a teenager, invited me out to lunch and gave me a check before we even ate. Sometimes it was $10, a couple of times it was $100, but ALMOST EVERY DAY FOR THREE WEEKS (until I got to my next revival, where the church took good care of me) money came in from somewhere. Usually, it was just enough to meet the urgent need of that day, with no idea how we would get through the next day. The next day there was money from another source, enough for that day. I felt like the widow of Zarephath who always had enough meal and oil for that day—I wondered if that barrel was ever full, but I KNOW it was never empty.*

During that time, a group of people from our home church quietly took up a collection among themselves (with my pastor's blessing) and brought a BIG check to my wife back home. Oh, and I must add that a door opened to preach somewhere on ALL of the four Sundays I had open, and a pastor invited me to run a revival at a church where I had never ministered, with less than three weeks' notice. As most any evangelist knows, that is almost miraculous, too.

One more thing before I shut up (cyber-ly speaking) I want to tell any evangelists who are new to this ministry (most of those who have been around for a while have more stories than I do) that in times of financial difficulty— which may be most of the time— always focus on Who your Provider is. A church where you minister is not your provider, your mailing list is not your provider, your job, or your spouse's, is not your provider. All of those will come up short from time to time, but if Jehovah Jirah is your Provider, He is the God of INFINITE Provision—even MIRACULOUS provision sometimes. So, don't get bent out of shape at a church that doesn't meet its responsibility to you as an evangelist—they are NOT your provider anyway. And if you really believe everything in that Bible you're preaching (and I believe it says exactly what God intended for it to say; that it is infallible, inerrant, and immutable) then quit wondering if you're going to be able to stay on the road or not. You will be out there preaching as long as God wants you to if you will keep your eyes on Him.

> "YOU WILL BE OUT THERE PREACHING AS LONG AS GOD WANTS YOU TO IF YOU WILL KEEP YOUR EYES ON HIM." -TC

CLOSING THOUGHTS

I hope that some of the advice from the field has been beneficial to you. The contributors listed at the end of this chapter have been on the field for several years. Although some are new to the evangelistic field and others have retired or moved into other areas of ministry, it is apparent that they have been in ministry for quite some time.

As culture and its challenges change from year to year, you will need to continually pray for God's divine counsel and wisdom to help you stay relevant as an evangelist. Even then, there will be times when you know that without God's intervention you will have to leave the field. It is at that point, when you have your back against the wall, that you will see God's divine provision in your own life.

Because when it is all said and done—it's really all about the calling of God. If He called you, He will make a way. It may not be your way or the way others have gone—but it will be God's direction for you and the ministry He has called you to embrace.

May His grace continually rest upon you, His hedge of protection envelope you and your loved ones, His hand guide and bless your ministry, and His Spirit work miracles through you....and that you would continually give Him all the honor due His name.

His servant,

Marshall M. Windsor, D. Min.

Many thanks to the following evangelist contributors:

David Copeland, Dustin Miller, Dan Montgomery, Justin Fennell, Marshall Windsor, Pete Olson, Sam Austin, Tim Collins, Tim Enloe

CHAPTER 9

The Pentecostal Dynamic

Traveling the gravel road, I thought I was surely lost. Some longtime friends of mine had invited me to join them at an old-time brush arbor revival meeting in northwest Arkansas, and I was trying my best to follow their directions. This was a day of no cell phones, and I had to rely on the only directions I had written down before leaving for the revival.

I was excited, yet a little nervous, about what to expect at my first brush arbor meeting, but I knew my friends would watch out for me since they acted as a couple of spiritual parents for me. After traveling for about two hours on state roads and county roads, I turned off on the appropriate gravel road. I traveled over a mile through the woods and around hairpin curves; and just when I thought I might have made a wrong turn, the road began to descend into a valley of sorts. When I came into the valley opening, I was shocked to find over one hundred RVs and campers lined up in rows with electric lines strung up all across the valley.

The roadway took me past the only church in the valley and a pole barn type structure that appeared to have sawdust or wood chips on the ground. I drove around the side of the church and was able to find my friends' RV—I had arrived at the brush arbor revival campgrounds, and I was about to get an education in Pentecost.

SOME FOUNDATION

If we want to gain a little education in Pentecost and our Pentecostal experience, we'll need to visit the biblical Book of Acts. This book was the second of a two-volume set originally known as the History of Christian Origins. They were considered complete in and of themselves and they contained the history of the first church era. The first volume of this set was separated and became known as the Gospel of Luke. The second volume became known as the book of Acts, or "The Acts of the Apostles." Written between 61 and 63 A.D., the authorship is attributed to Luke.

This is due to the use of many medical terms, external witnesses, and mainly, the internal evidence of the "we" passages in Acts 16 and 20. The setting appears to be Rome while Luke is with Paul, and Luke seems to be writing to confirm the faith of a certain Theophilus. In doing so, he shows the mission of the church, God's sovereign plan of redemption to Jews and Gentiles, the saving work of Jesus Christ and the power of the Holy Spirit.

Pentecostal folks get a lot of their support from Acts, 1:8; 2:4; Chapters 10 and 19; along with Joel 2:28, wherein God states through his prophet Joel that He will pour out His Spirit upon all flesh in the latter days. Acts 1:8 became somewhat of an index of contents for the Book of Acts. First, the disciples were told to be witnesses in Jerusalem (Chapters 1-7), then in Judaea and Samaria (chapters 8, 9), and then to the end of the earth (Chapters 10 to the end of Acts). The main significance was that the mission of the disciples was now without geographical limitations—as it is to every Christian today.

Every evangelist (and Pentecostal Christian for that matter) must realize that the Pentecostal experience, known as the Baptism in the Holy Spirit or Holy Spirit Baptism, was given to empower us for service. Jesus told the disciples to wait for the promise of the Father in Acts 1:4, 5. Jesus also said in Acts 1:8, that they would receive power when the Holy Spirit was come upon them, and to wait in Jerusalem until they received this power (Luke 24:49). This is not regeneration or sanctification because all other scriptures reveal that we must repent, be baptized (or show our belief publicly), and then receive the promise of the Holy Spirit (as in Peter's message in Acts 2:38). You may not feel a tremendous surge in physical power since this is spiritual in nature, but you will gain revelation of God's Word and an increased ability to overcome sin in your life. You may also gain a heightened level of spiritual discernment.

But, what does Pentecost have to do with this Pentecostal dynamic? Well, Pentecost was better known as the Feast of Weeks or Feast of Pentecost. It was the second great festival within the Jewish calendar in which God's people lifted up the first fruits of grain harvest to Him. Pentecost eventually became the ceremony to commemorate the giving of the Law at Mt. Sinai as well. The word, Pentecost, meant "fifty" because it took place fifty days after Passover.

On the day of Pentecost, the disciples were gathered in an upper room when the power of Pentecost descended upon them like "tongues of fire." They "were all filled with the Holy Spirit and began to speak in other tongues as the Spirit gave them utterance" (Acts. 2:4, ESV). This initial physical evidence of speaking in other tongues evidenced the empowerment of Pentecost. Today, when people talk about the Pentecostal dynamic, they are talking about the supernatural empowerment of the Holy Spirit that equips the church to fulfill its mission to the world.

MY STORY

So, let me get back to my initial story with my friends. After our hellos and hugs, I settled in with my friends and prepared to enjoy the services that night. As the time for service drew close, we headed to the pole barn structure. A time of worship ensued, but nothing spectacular seemed to be happening in my opinion. Then, an older lady on the stage began to play her guitar and sing this song all by herself: "This heart of mine, this heart of mine. The Lord has changed this heart of mine. Now I can walk right, and I can talk right, 'cause the Lord has changed this heart of mine." She continued singing, and an older gentleman began dancing and shuffling around in front of that platform where the lady was singing.

While I stood there listening to a song I'd never heard and watching a man dance "in the Spirit," I must say I was a bit captivated like a youngster in his or her first trip to the candy store. But, the crowd began to shout out praises to God and the volume of praises began to crescendo. All at once it seemed like people were shouting and praying and praising God. The presence of God was so thick that I didn't know what to do. The pastor led the people to form a prayer line, and we all seemed to go through it.

Many people were falling under the power of the Holy Spirit and found themselves lost in the presence of God. I was even invited to help pray with people with my friends and some of them fell under the power of God's presence. It was truly an education to someone who had never been in a service like that before.

The wonderful thing about that experience is that it was followed by the preaching of God's Word—the Scriptures—and after the service, I was able to talk about all that happened with my older friends who were used to this kind of Pentecostal service. But not every Pentecostal-type service is a great service. There are those who prey on others and use the guise of being spiritual to lay hands on people and manipulate them. We all have to remember that the Church on this side of Heaven is not a perfect Church—it's full of fallen people who, for the most part, are honestly trying to live a Christ-like life. That's why we need discernment and wisdom when embracing the Pentecostal dynamic of ministry.

During this same revival meeting, the pastor conducted Sunday services in the church. During one altar call, a man came up to me, laid his hands on me, and started prophesying over me. He said something to the effect that I was in a dry, desert place but he saw "in the spirit" there was a pool of water at my feet and God was beginning to pour out rivers of living water in my life and ministry. He said that the pool of water was growing and everything the water touched became green and fruitful.

You would think that would have blessed me immeasurably, but in reality, I felt such a grieving in my soul and spirit that all I wanted to do was cry. It was the most terrible feeling I think I had ever had up to that point. I went to my friends and told them what happened and asked them to pray for me. They prayed for quite some time and then the burden lifted. I pointed the man out to my friends, and they said that they had been following him around and praying for the people after he prayed for them. I never realized at that point that allowing other people to pray for you could be a bad thing—but it surely was that day.

Why do I share all this? It's because you need to realize that you must never allow the presence and power of the Holy Spirit be seen as a stamp of approval on your, or anyone else's, lifestyle. Pentecostal people love to worship freely, and sometimes we see that freedom as the liberation that comes with a sinless or forgiven life. There is most certainly forgiveness in Jesus Christ as 1 John 1:9 tells us, but I've seen great Pentecostal services that ended with people heading to their cars to smoke a cigarette and cursing with their friends—that's not Christlikeness.

In a Pentecostal service, folks try to be sensitive to the leading of the Holy Spirit, and that is truly a good thing. We should be led of the Spirit as Pentecostals. But we must also be grounded in the Word of God. Others can manipulate our emotions if we are not careful. It is refreshing and reviving when the Holy Spirit leads us, but when we're led by a man or woman to do Pentecostal activities, it will wear you out. I've seen Jericho marches, people jumping, shouting, shaking, laughing, singing in the spirit, and numerous other outward expressions of the Holy Spirit touching lives in an incredible way. But I've also seen other people perform these actions with their eyes wide open and looking around—hoping to attract attention to themselves.

No matter what happens in a true Pentecostal service, it should all seek to glorify God. The true Holy Spirit of God will glorify the Father.

Jesus said in Matthew 5:16 (NIV), "In the same way, let your light shine before others, that they may see your good deeds and glorify your Father in Heaven."

Paul told the Romans in Romans 15:5-6, "May the God who gives endurance and encouragement give you the same attitude of mind toward each other that Christ had so that with one mind and one voice you may glorify the God and Father of our Lord Jesus Christ." Any Pentecostal experience that exalts a man or woman is not the true Holy Spirit because Scripture tells us in Isaiah 42:8 (KJV), "I am the Lord: that is my name: and my glory will I not give to another, neither my praise to graven images."

LOOKING BACK TO AZUSA

A great example for us can be found in William J. Seymour, an African-American brother, who led the Azusa Street Revival back in the early 1900s. William H. Durham has this to say about brother Seymour: "He walks and talks with God. His power is in his weakness. He seems to maintain a helpless dependence on God and is as simple-hearted as a little child, and at the same time is so filled with God that you feel the love and power every time you get near him."[15] That's what the Pentecostal dynamic can do in your ministry if you let it. It can lead you into such an intimate relationship with God that you can not only have a greater sensitivity to His leading during your times of ministry, but others will instantly realize that the humility, love, and power of God Himself flow through your personal life as well.

As a Pentecostal minister, one of the hardest battles you will fight is pride. William Seymour is a great example of humility for every Christian and minister of the Gospel of Jesus Christ. It is said that he would often be seen kneeling in prayer before the Lord during services

---

15 Cecil M. Robeck, Jr., *The Azusa Street Mission And Revival: The Birth of the Global Pentecostal Movement* (Nashville: Nelson, 2006), 91.

with his head in a wooden crate. That ought to be a vivid reminder that pride is a constant spiritual battle. We should fight to deflect every bit of praise people heap on us to the Giver of every good and perfect gift (James 1:17). Once we start taking the credit for God's work in our meetings, we'll begin to feel the pressure to perform so that great manifestations will continue to be a part of our ministries. But, the reality is that it is not our ministry—it's God's.

Thankfully, the Pentecostal experience offers a prayer language for the believer to tarry in prayer, even when he or she does not know for what to pray. A witness of William Seymour's ministry and prayer life stated: "Before arriving in Los Angeles, Seymour had committed himself to the personal discipline of spending five or more hours each day in prayer."[16] This seems almost a superhuman feat, especially considering today's fast-paced society.

However, the example Seymour displayed reveals a lot about his character and the preeminence that prayer should have in our ministries today. If evangelists truly believe God has called them to Pentecostal ministry, then they must maintain a vibrantly intimate relationship with God. Since Jesus is the only soul-winner, evangelists must foster and protect their prayer life because it remains the lifeline of every "successful" ministry. The supernatural should be a normative part of every Pentecostal service instead of the rare exception that it has become today.

The Pentecostal experience led a renewed sense of mission for the Church at large—especially on Azusa Street. The Azusa Street Mission's four-step process of immediately trying to discern a language and missionary calling following an individual's baptism in the Spirit experience reflects Seymour's convictions of Christ's soon coming and the Church's mission to win the lost.

During the peak years of the Azusa Street revival, many missionaries classified themselves as "missionary evangelists" as they embarked upon

---

16 Robeck, Jr., 93.

their missionary calling by itinerating to raise needed travel funds throughout the United States. The Azusa Street missionary program initiated what historian, Vinson Synan, described as "the one-way ticket." Christ's return loomed so near that a return ticket from the mission field almost appeared as a lack of faith.

LEADING PENTECOSTAL-LY AS EVANGELISTS

As I contemplated the concept of leading Pentecostal-ly, I initially had visions of "old-time Pentecost" with beehive hairdos and separation of men and women during after-service fellowship dinners. My earlier story alludes to these types of scenarios. Albeit to me, the real heart of Pentecostal leadership for the evangelist lies in trusting God emphatically and leaning upon the Holy Spirit's "gifts" to lead in Pentecostal fashion.

Personally, I feel everyone has some capacity for leadership. Leadership involves "leading" and if we have the ability to lead someone to Christ, then we have the capacity to lead. Many people obviously flee from leadership opportunities, opting for the easier route of letting someone else step up to the plate. But the truth remains, we are made in the image of God and that image includes the capacity to lead—helping us fulfill our obligation in the "Great Commission."

In order for me to work through my perspective on leading Pentecostal-ly, I must look back once again. This is not an autobiography, but merely a glance over my shoulder, revealing the lens through which I see and setting the stage for future insights. This lens has journeyed through varied forges: shaped by family, denominations, divine appointments and, hopefully, the Holy Spirit.

In my take of leading Pentecostal-ly, I want to share some insights surrounding our increased sensitivity, boldness, divine communication, as well as the "make it happen" "let it happen" tension—revealing some of the value Pentecostals bring to the table. Our "fruit" will obviously be the major element validating the need and place for Pentecostal evangelists today, but also hopefully opening the door to greater influence and position within the Church at large.

MY LENS

I strongly believe that the Pentecostal experience does not change who we are or the value systems we have held throughout our lives, but that it does enhance and utilize them. As a matter of fact, most people today can testify how their salvation experience stands as the catalyst, which made such an obvious transformation in their lives. We have seen drug addicts and alcoholics delivered, violent folks transformed with new personas, and even life-long prostitutes now living wonderful married lives with children. God truly renovates our lives in that moment when he indwells a new vessel. Even individuals who have lived wonderful lives gain a fullness they did not previously enjoy upon entrance into God's family.

I say that to emphasize the importance of our early forming years in life. The lens through which I viewed life took shape in the early years of my middle-class life on a central Missouri farm. I learned the value of a dollar and hard work. I learned that a man's word was his bond and a handshake carried more weight than any legal document.

Integrity and honesty were the backbone of whatever else I was, but it was God's divine presence that radically sharpened my moral compass. My previous military service only helped emphasize the value of honor, courage, and country. So, the lens through which I embody Pentecost may vary distinctly from someone forged by different family values, culture, or even language.

Being raised Southern Baptist also brought its own set of biases, as well as positive influences. Through the help of the Southern Baptist's Master Life Discipleship program, and a little help from my Pentecostal brother, I came into Pentecost. When I began a search for the deeper things of God, I never realized that it would lead to a personal Pentecost. After all, I thought Pentecostals were weird—and now I am one. That said, I cannot see that my Pentecostal experience changed my value system. However, it does exist as a catalyst through which I strategically capitalize on my core values—values which remain a defining part of my life.

Part of being a good leader lies in willingly working hard and taking the initiative necessary that will help add value to others and exert our influence for positive results. Finding what needs to be done and "doing it" seems to characterize most prominent leaders and evangelists today.

So, bringing hard work and initiative into the spiritual realm in no way denigrates their need in building great leadership traits, but actually enhances our spiritual leadership. The foundational key to good Pentecostal evangelistic leadership lies in utilizing Pentecostal distinctives to lead at a higher level via the Holy Spirit's guidance. Leading Pentecostal-ly as evangelists demands sensitivity to the voice of God, who obviously embodies the perfect Leader.

So, while Pentecostal evangelists and leaders have the opportunity to glean valuable insights and training from secular society, we must channel these insights through the biblical lens as well. We have heard some of the clichés surrounding leadership, like "leaders are learners" and "leaders are readers" just to name a couple, but spiritual leadership must ground these virtues on the foundation of God's Word if leaders intend to survive and thrive in today's church.

William Seymour would shudder at the thought that "we" can do this because it reeks of selfishness and pride. A foundation upon God and His Word remain paramount; and because Pentecostal people enjoy a greater sensitivity to the Holy Spirit, Pentecostal leadership can run amuck if not solidly grounded in the Word of God. Our contribution to the "art of leadership" can be seen in the value added through the biblically based guidance of the Holy Spirit; not only in leading the Church at large as Pentecostal evangelists, but also directing our own personal lives.

MY TAKE

A Greater Sensitivity

An interesting caveat in my personal experience has helped form my opinions concerning the spiritually led Pentecostal evangelist. My entrance into Pentecost came with quite a contrast since I was not raised up in the Pentecostal arena. Shortly after my "baptism in the Holy Spirit" experience, a greater sensitivity to the spiritual realm became evident. I vividly remember how the very words of Scripture seemed to leap off the page at me when reading my Bible. Others have testified to similar occurrences along with an intimacy with God unlike anything previously experienced. A "presence" of the Holy Spirit guided them on a daily basis.

Like hair flying in the breeze or even the webs of newly hatched spiders carried along by the wind, aptly depicted in the movie *Charlotte's Web*, we also seem guided along life's path. Instead of only hearing God when he shouts or straining for the still small voice of God, or running into walls along a dark corridor, the Pentecostal believer can even hear God when He whispers—if so desired. Life does get noisy, and Pentecostals can be just as guilty as any other believer of allowing the noise of life to drown out the Spirit's leading.

Every Pentecostal evangelist and leader should feel the mandate to passionately pursue God's guidance in every aspect of his or her ministry. I do not mean to insinuate that other spiritual leaders cannot hear from God or that they fail to seek God for his direction and wisdom. Every spiritual leader desires God's perfect will for their ministries and personal lives, but the intimacy that accompanies the Pentecostal remains particular to those embracing a "baptism" experience.

A Greater Boldness

A special endowment, or greater filling of the Holy Spirit, is what characterizes the Pentecostal person; and an "evangelist" with this endowment gains a greater boldness, and even gifting, to lead where the

Holy Spirit directs. In Numbers eleven we can see how the Holy Spirit came upon the elders in order to help Moses in the leadership role of God's people. God gave a special enabling of His Holy Spirit necessary to lead God's people, which should be seen as a basic requirement for Pentecostal leadership and normative for every Pentecostal believer.

If we really believe Acts chapter one, then we hold fast to God's purpose for Pentecost—the reception of power for ministry. We hold fast to the significance of this "enduement" of power for service because something supernatural happens that emboldens all of us for some level of leadership within God's Church. While I agree this level of boldness has been reserved for those baptized in the Spirit, sadly many are still fearful and in the closet with their faith.

So often believers are afraid, not ashamed, to share what God has done in their lives. Pentecostal evangelists and leaders have the challenge of modeling an emboldened lifestyle because God's people still need a model who will lead with humility and boldness—just like Moses.

This is so true today, especially when thinking about how we as Pentecostal leaders "do" evangelism. We must find ways within the culture setting where God has placed us that will effectively reach those "outside" the faith, then emulate that method of evangelism and motivate our people to do the same. Although there is something to be said about filling the pulpit and letting God take care of filling the pew, we need to proactively engage our communities for the sake of the Gospel. As we involve ourselves in positive ways, walls and stereotypes will fall, while raising opportunities to show the reality of Christ in our day-to-day lives.

Boldness, in and of itself, cannot be the all-inclusive earmark of a Pentecostal evangelist, or leader, because we can look around us in any direction and see boldness exemplified within the non-Pentecostal sectors as well. But a certain measure of boldness must be a part of every evangelist. The Pentecostal evangelist, however, can tap into the heavenly resources through a language, not his or her own, and at times enjoys supernatural boldness that God unleashes at His discretion. The Pentecostal evangelist has access to a special communication with God, which non-Pentecostals do not enjoy, opening up a whole arsenal of heavenly resources.

A Greater Communication

This divine communication probably reflects the greatest area of "visible" contrast between the Pentecostal evangelist and leader and their evangelical counterparts. Praying "in the Spirit," also known as divine utterance, allows us ample opportunity to "pray without ceasing" as well as pray when we don't know how to pray. Communicating with our Heavenly Father in a way only understandable by Him remains a mystery to most, but an invaluable tool as a Pentecostal leader. The ability to pray, even when we do not know how to pray, opens doors of understanding, helps us gain victory during spiritual battles, and even refreshes us in ways that only God can initiate.

As the National Evangelists' Representative for the Assemblies of God, I lean heavily on the Holy Spirit for wisdom, guidance, discernment, and courage. I represent multiple itinerant ministries and/or evangelists, and I need God's direction in all that I do. I cannot always satisfy everyone I represent; neither can I disregard the authority under which I serve. I also cannot definitively know exactly how to pray in every situation I face—I must rely on my prayer language to help guide me in praying for our evangelists and the national office initiatives that will best benefit them. Whether I teach seminars, facilitate national conferences, produce educational materials or just try to maneuver through some political terrain, God's revelation and direction remain a constant need as well as a wonderful source of comfort and courage.

Politics abound even in the church and can cripple the Pentecostal evangelist or leader if not traversed correctly. Robert Quinn states, "Learning how to act appropriately and to cope effectively in the political environment is extremely important."[17] This has been something I have

---

17 Robert E. Quinn, *Deep Change: Discovering the Leader Within* (San Francisco: Jossey-Bass, 1996), 112.

experienced first-hand and struggled with often. The adjustment from evangelist - to office staff - to department head has definitely been a transition from technical expertise to political prowess. Most of us receive our "promotions" if you will, through technical expertise, but our promotion often moves us into the political environment of leadership.

I have always avoided politics, so this adjustment has necessitated a deep change within me in order for me to function and flourish as a Pentecostal leader within an often political arena. Unfortunately, this change came with lots of anger, tears, prayer and God's grace; a change that came through divine communication on an intimate level with God in order to truly hear his voice and not my own.

As an itinerant evangelist, I often pray for people at the altar areas located near the pulpit when a service concludes. In praying for others, I completely rely on the Holy Spirit to lead me in how I should pray. I often find myself praying "in the spirit" with my heavenly language as I seek God for that individual and their needs. When "excesses" begin to surface, I also turn to the Holy Spirit in prayer for wisdom and discernment on the proper course of action to take.

An illustration of this happened recently while in revival services at Assemblée Chrétienne du Nord in St-Jérôme, Quebec, Canada. Many people received prayer during the altar invitation, and as I often do, I utilized a mixture of English and my prayer language while praying for the needs of others. While I stood chatting with the pastor and associate pastor after this wonderful altar service, a young man came up to ask us a question. He asked, in a rhetorical way through the interpreter, whether I understood the tongues I had spoken while praying for him. He thought that if tongues were spoken there should have been an interpretation. This was a sincere question and one that would obviously have an impact on him.

I was able to share how the Bible talks about the "gift of tongues," which necessitates interpretation because it is a message of edification or correction to the church; and the prayer language, which every

"Pentecostal" believer can, and should, utilize. I shared the necessity of my prayer language in this instance because I did not know exactly how to pray for him—I needed the Holy Spirit to show me. I was not speaking a "word from the Lord" for him; I was merely praying out loud while seeking the Lord's direction concerning how to pray. I needed to hear from God concerning specific issues I should pray for in his life.

I appreciated the boldness of this young man to come and ask us about this situation, which apparently troubled him. Through his questions, I realized two things: tongues can easily cause confusion, and leading Pentecostal-ly involves our need to pray in the Spirit in order to communicate with God for His leading. As Pentecostal evangelists and leaders, we need to maintain sensitivity to the non-Pentecostal as we minister in order to help maintain order within the church and diminish confusion, which is not of God. I like to tell non-Pentecostal visitors in our services that Pentecostals just enjoy a freer expression of their passion for Jesus Christ, but it should not be something that distracts us from what God wants to do in our lives.

Pentecostal evangelists and leaders need this intimate communication because we often find ourselves in unfamiliar territory—operating out of our "comfort zone." But even when we are on familiar ground, or so we think, the Pentecostal's prayer language provides access to a level of communication not available to others. This cannot be the cause for a "better than you" attitude, but reveals the wonderful opportunity and responsibility we have, as Pentecostals, to know God's will in each of our situations. We have a privileged relationship with our Heavenly Father—a relationship marked by divine communication.

THE "LET IT HAPPEN" "MAKE IT HAPPEN" TENSION

Pentecostals have always desired a "leading" of the Holy Spirit in all that they do, and the Pentecostal evangelist especially so; albeit, there has always been a "pragmatic" side of ministry. While some have tried to hide this aspect of ministry, most ministers seeking selfish gain often find their ministries drying up over the years. Interestingly, one's background plays a huge role in their attitude—especially financial stewardship. Those coming out of poverty have different issues than those coming from an affluent background.

A case in point can be seen in my feeling of responsibility to help alleviate the financial pressures of itinerant ministers. Finances appear to be one of the main determining factors in those ministers turning their ministries into a business, and those endeavoring to hear the voice of God in all things—especially finances. Financial pressures tend to bring out character shortcomings, allowing manipulation techniques and other ministerial atrocities to surface in otherwise wonderful servants of God.

The tension between "let it happen" and "make it happen" can be unbearable when the financial stresses rise—and we always strive to justify whichever action we feel inclined to pursue. The more I prayed about this tension, the more I sensed God revealing that this is just a normal part of ministry—whether you are a pastor or evangelist.

This tension led me to appreciate Dr. Roger Cotton's leadership principles discovered in Numbers chapter eleven. When trouble and stressors rise in our lives, we have an initial tendency to look inward for the answers. But as Cotton so articulately pointed out, the answers for God's church lie in "God and His Spirit working in and through us."[18] Perhaps that's why William Seymour prayed so much. As fallen people struggling to take up our cross daily and crucifying our fleshly desires, our answers will always mirror something less than perfection. However, God has graciously chosen to use broken, fallen vessels to carry out his plan. The very vessels needing grace have been called

---

18 Roger D. Cotton, "Numbers 11 and a Pentecostal Theology of Church Leadership," *Encounter: Journal for Pentecostal Ministry*, Summer 2004, Vol.1, No.1 [journal on-line]; available from http://www.agts.edu/encounter/articles/2004_summer/ cotton.htm; Internet; accessed 23 January 2016.

likewise to lead God's people and embrace the empowering Pentecostal experience on a daily basis.

As a Pentecostal, the "baptism" in the Holy Spirit comes upon an individual as they "totally abandon" themselves to the Holy Spirit's infilling. It is the "total abandonment" that allows one to receive the Pentecostal experience and it is this abandonment which allows one to continually seek a greater sensitivity and leading from the Holy Spirit.

The tension comes when we try to take control back from the initial abandonment of our lives to God for a greater leading by His Holy Spirit. Interestingly, we seek to have a greater sense of God's presence in our personal lives and as the Holy Spirit leads us we endeavor to pursue His leading with all that is within us. So, the more you seek God, the more you "want" to seek Him—quite an intriguing paradox, but one that has proven itself time and time again. Although one could argue that any believer should have this compulsion, the Pentecostal minister should have an exponential enabling of, and passion for, God's Holy Spirit.

It is the "enabling" that allows us to "let it happen" within the confines of Scripture. Any leader knows that guidance and correction are a part of leadership. The Pentecostal evangelist and leader is attuned to the Spirit's leading so that he or she will understand not just what is happening in the physical, but more importantly, what is happening in the spiritual realm. Pentecostal leaders must continually nurture an intimate relationship with God so they can step in to correct and "make it happen," or step back to "let it happen" when needed.

MINISTERING HOLY SPIRIT BAPTISM

I won't talk at length here because there are several folks around whose ministry emphasizes this wonderful dynamic of the Holy Spirit (check the online evangelist directory for that emphasis at http://evangelists. ag.org/directory). They would be great folks to call, and I'm sure they would be thrilled to give advice. Much prayer is key, sensitivity to the Holy Spirit as well as to those people who are seeking is vital, and giving clear direction to those seeking on what to expect is very important. The Holy Spirit won't make them speak (there may be rare exceptions of powerful baptisms but it does not seem like this is the norm). The Baptism is like a "deeper breath" (as one author states) of what they already have—the Holy Spirit.

One evangelist shared that Acts 19:6 is the text they use to minister the Baptism with the Holy Spirit, but there are many ways to launch some teaching on the Baptism of the Holy Spirit. Ministry leaders do a great job of repetitive teaching on salvation, rightly so, and how to restore that heavenly relationship with our Creator, God. However, we sadly expect people to just "get it" when the invitation is given to receive prayer for this gift of the Holy Spirit baptism.

Many great books have been written about this gift: like Dr. Stanley Horton's "What the Bible Says About the Holy Spirit;" Dr. Anthony D. Palma's "The Holy Spirit: A Pentecostal Perspective;" Tim Enloe's "Want More?" and Dr. Doyle Jones' "Be Filled With The Spirit." The reality is that we should focus on what our part is in the process and realize the Holy Spirit will do His part.

People seeking usually need a lot of encouragement—older folks have more hurdles to cross with preconceived ideas and past missed opportunities. A major ingredient for any baptism is a hunger for God—not the Baptism. You can either pray for folks individually or ask certain folks that regularly pray in their heavenly language to pray for their friends—many times people will trust their friends and let down their guard that they may have with a stranger (evangelist). Mass baptisms are another scenario altogether—for crusade events. But, no matter what venue or occasion presents itself, the Pentecostal dynamic is an experience that God wants every believer to receive. So, if you know folks who have been seeking for a long time, encourage them, teach them, pray for them, and help them tear down any hindrances that may be present.

SOME CONCLUDING THOUGHTS

When God's presence shows up in a powerful way, often during prayer following a service, excesses often arise if you are not careful. It appears as though certain individuals receive a "green light" to let it all hang out—and sometimes that can be ugly. As evangelists, we must have the leading of the Holy Spirit, revealing the crucial need for that Pentecostal dynamic—allowing us to communicate with God on an intensely intimate level. The utterance gifts are obviously important and are crucial in exposing God's people to the full counsel of God, but Pentecostal evangelists must pursue the ability to lead and act in the middle of the manifest presence of God—especially during services— with God's Pentecostal empowerment.

Leading Pentecostal-ly as an evangelist means you and I must embrace a greater sensitivity and boldness, through divine communication, and abandonment to the Holy Spirit that enables us to boldly advance the Kingdom of God and not man. The utterance gifts are an additional resource, enabling the Spirit empowered evangelist greater opportunities of discernment and direction in an even greater capacity than our evangelical brothers and sisters. God's spiritual gifts—including the baptism in the Holy Spirit—are not meant to be divisive within the global Church, but an arsenal of God's resources to help spread the Gospel of Jesus Christ. When we allow selflessness and the other fruits of the spirit to flourish, while guided by God's divine presence, evangelists will reflect the kind of Pentecostal leadership necessary for the Church today.

A MESSAGE FROM A FRIEND

When I stumbled upon this message by Dr. Gary A. Denbow (my former pastor who married Nancy and me), I felt the Holy Spirit prompt me to include it in this chapter. Dr. Denbow and his family spent many distinguished years as a missionary to the Philippines, church pastor, President of Central Bible College, and director of missions at North

Central University prior to his retirement. There is no other person I respect more and who has encouraged me to stay in the fight when it was the last thing I wanted to do. I pray that this sample message on the value of our Pentecostal witness will be a blessing to you and give you some ideas on preaching about the Pentecostal distinctive of Holy Spirit baptism. The message was preached to Bible school students and faculty in chapel on January 27, 2010.

WE VALUE A PENTECOSTAL WITNESS

Luke 24:48; Acts 1:4-8

Central Bible College   **27 January 2010**
Dr. Gary A. Denbow, President

There are a lot of ways to say goodbye. Here are a few recognizable ones.

- Live long and prosper (Trekkie)
- May the force be with you (Star Wars)
- Hasta la vista, baby (Terminator)
- Andiamo, Bambini (The Fugitive)
- If you need me, all you have to do is whistle (To Have/Have Not)
- To the Batmobile... (Batman)
- Goodnight, you princes of Maine, you kings of New England (Cider House Rules)

But Jesus did not choose one of those. Instead, He chose to give His closest followers the clearest of directions. He chose to outline for them His wishes first for the next ten days and then for the days until His return. Notice what He beckoned His followers to do. He told them as though He was giving step-by-step instructions.

STEP ONE: WAIT (Acts 1:4)

Jesus had a plan for disbursing His disciples into the entire world. Every step would prove extremely valuable. None should be avoided. The first thing He commanded was for His disciples to wait right there in Jerusalem. And my first question must be why did they have to wait?

1. There were business issues that faced them. A leader had fallen. They felt it their responsibility to go through the process of choosing a new one.
2. There were strong personalities among the disciples. We know that 120 of them gathered together. They all brought their own agenda to the meeting. I am sure it took a day or two for all of them to concentrate on just one thing—the promise of Jesus to them. They had to be in "one accord."
3. I am also sure that each of the 120 had personal issues. Peter, James, John, Thomas, and Phillip all entered the upper room having filtered Jesus' message through their own understanding. Perhaps, at the beginning of their prayer meeting, there was even strife over songs or styles or orders of worship. It would take a few days in prayer before all the disciples had worked through personality issues and were seeking the same thing.
4. Waiting builds anticipation. A very valuable gift is worth waiting for. What Jesus promised would be life-changing and well worth the wait.

STEP TWO: EXPECT

Their waiting was to be with expectation. Jesus had made them a promise that He intended to fulfill. He wanted them to stay right where they were and receive the promise of the Holy Spirit baptism. The truth was that they did not know exactly what they were waiting for or just how they were to receive the promise.

And that had to be hard. Don't you know it was a subject of conversation? But, had they just thought, Jesus had given them a fairly good picture.

- The promise was of another (of the same kind) counselor (advocate) who would never leave them (John 14:16).
- The promise was of a divine Teacher who would reveal to them the truth about God, just as Jesus in the flesh had done (John 14:26).
- The promise was of One who would constantly remind them of Christ, Himself (John 15:26-27).
- The promise was of One who would convict and convince everyone of the evils of sin and the righteousness of God (John 16:8).
- The promise was of One who would guide them into all truth (John 16:13).

STEP THREE: CONCENTRATE

They immediately began to insert their own questions into the debate. They wanted a timeline for end-time events. They wanted questions answered about their own futures. Jesus' words are a mild rebuke to them. It was not their prerogative to know the times and epochs that were a part of God's plan. They were asking the wrong questions. They had to be brought back to the present need that each of them had—they did not have the power of the Holy Spirit, and they simply could not do God's work without it.

STEP FOUR: RECEIVE

Jesus' intention for them was that they would wait for a time and, then, they would receive the promised Holy Spirit and power. He did not say how long they were to wait in terms of days. It turned out to be ten days.

But He did say what would end their waiting. They were to receive. They were not to grab, appropriate, catch, or run after the blessing promised. They were just to receive that promise.

That had to be hard. So much of what they had been taught about worship led them to believe that worship was action: selecting a sacrifice, killing and burning the sacrifice, etc. Not this time. They were to wait, expect, and receive the greatest blessing they could ever hope for, but they couldn't earn it, or pay for it, or work for it. They could only receive it.

STEP FIVE: GO

The immediate result of receiving the Holy Spirit power would be that they would be deployed to the ends of the earth with a single task—they would be His witnesses—they would testify about Him—they would speak for Him.

1. They were to go because there was nothing for which to stay. I am very fond of *A Biblical Theology of Missions* by Dr. George W. Peters, long-time professor of missions at Dallas Theological Seminary. He introduced me to the idea of the difference in the centripetal effect of the Jewish religion—it brought people to Jerusalem because Jerusalem was the place of salvation—and the centrifugal effect of the Christian religion—it drove people from Jerusalem.

2. Harry Boer: *Pentecost and Missions,* puts it this way: "The profound effect which Pentecost had on the life and work of the Church is underscored and grows in clarity when we contrast the New Testament *ekklesia* with the Old Testament *kahal* (congregation). A farther-reaching change in the constitution of a religious community is hardly conceivable than that which Pentecost affected in the internal and external structure in and through which the life of the people of God expressed itself. Up to Pentecost the central place of worship had been the temple; the central office-bearer, the priest; the central cultic object, the altar; the central cultic act, sacrifice. With the coming of the Spirit, this entire cultic complex was abrogated. For a while, the members of the *ekklesia* continued to have a place in the *kahal,* but this dual loyalty was a transitional phenomenon. Pentecost was the death-knell of temple, priest, altar, sacrifice, law, and ceremony. All of it

disappeared, and in their place, came the preaching of the Gospel and the sacraments, together bearing witness to the completed work of Christ. 'With the coming of the Church, Jerusalem no longer has any function…the fall of Jerusalem and the sending out of the apostles into the world—this is the end of the old covenant and the beginning of the Gospel.' *At Pentecost, a reconstitution of the Church took place, which changed the Old Testament sacerdotal kahal into the witnessing ekklesia of the New.* The true worship of the Father would henceforth take place neither in Jerusalem nor on Mt. Gerizim, but it would be exercised in spirit and in truth wherever the Gospel is preached and believingly accepted. When the great High Priest had brought His sacrifice on the altar of the cross, there was no longer room for the ministry of types and shadows that had foretold His coming. There remained but one task: Witness to His completed work. The veil of the temple had been rent and the middle wall of partition dividing Jew and Gentile taken away."

3. Jerusalem no longer held them, and their fears no longer bound them. They were to become the greatest witnessing force the world had ever seen. Again, Dr. Boer: P. 109-110. "It may without exaggeration be said that the preponderance of emphasis in all that Jesus says about the coming Spirit, and the preponderance of emphasis in Luke's account of the coming of the Spirit at Pentecost and in his description of the missionary expansion of the Church in the remainder of Acts, lies on the witnessing activity of the Spirit and of the recipients of the Spirit. It is at Pentecost that the witness of the Church began, and it is in the power of the Pentecostal Spirit that this witness continues to be carried forward."

"The Scriptural emphasis of the work of the Holy Spirit is to confer life. The means He has selected to transmit life is the preaching of the Gospel. Therefore … "the witness of the Spirit in the proclamation of the Church is the basis out of which all the other activities of the Spirit in the Church take their rise."

"Therefore, the Church is first and last a witnessing, a proclaiming community."

APPLICATION

Does it not make sense that we should value what Christ valued if, indeed, we claim to be His ministers? Could He be any clearer about what He valued than to listen to His parting words? Our work is to internalize these steps that were so important to Christ—to adopt His plan as our core value. We value a Pentecostal witness to our world. So, let's rehearse Jesus' plan and apply it to our lives.

1. Wait. Processing time is hard for us. We are the generation that wants instant everything. Anything that takes time can't be worth the wait, can it? Think about this!
   - Every major biblical leader had a processing time. Some were short, and some were longer. It took Moses 40 years to get ready to go on the mission God had for him.
   - You and I have a prescribed processing time for our leadership capabilities to mature. First, education, Second, spiritual and emotional maturity. Third, internship. At some point, the Holy Spirit deems us ready and propels us out to be His witnesses.
   - Don't hate the processing time, embrace it instead.
2. Expect.
   - It is not hyper-faith or weird to just expect God to do exactly what He says. Don't let someone talk you out of God's best for your lives. If you read in the Word, and clearly understand what the message is to you, then appropriate that Word. What God says is what you are supposed to have.
   - Take Him at His Word. He will do just what He said He would. What someone else experienced does not negate the Word. Don't lower your expectations to meet someone's desires for you. Jesus is the giver of the Holy Spirit.
3. Concentrate.
   - Paul wrote to Timothy, "Timothy, guard what has been entrusted to you, avoiding worldly and empty chatter and the opposing arguments of what is falsely called

"knowledge" — which some have professed and thus gone astray from the faith" (1 Tim. 6:20-21).

- He wrote this to the Colossians. "Don't let anyone capture you with empty philosophies and high-sounding nonsense that come from human thinking and from the spiritual powers of this world, rather than from Christ" (Col. 2:8).

- Set your sights higher. "Therefore, if you have been raised up with Christ, keep seeking the things above, where Christ is, seated at the right hand of God. Set your mind on the things above, not on the things that are on Earth" (Col. 3:1-2).

4. Receive.

- Receive divine energy. Expect a baptism of power that will effectively energize all areas of your Christian service.

- Receive divine authority. Expect to receive not only the direction of the Lord for your life but also to receive the license to proceed into His harvest field for you.

- Receive divine companionship. He will not bid you to go where He will not lead you. He will not send you outside of His care. He will not thrust you out further than His hand can hold you.

5. Go.

- I love the contrast. Stay until the power comes, and then go.

- I love how the Lord used the circumstances in Jerusalem to thrust His disciples out. Acts 8:1 records that persecution scattered the disciples, but not the apostles.

- It took the power of the Holy Spirit to drive Peter to Joppa and then to Caesarea by the Sea.

- The disciples scattered to the four winds carrying the Gospel message. You can answer these questions.

  1. Did James, the brother of Jesus, die in Spain?
  2. Did the Apostle Thomas die in India?
  3. Did any of the original Twelve, except for James, the brother of John, die in Jerusalem, as far as we know?

- They all heard the direct command of Jesus Christ and went. That is still the imperative upon us. We must go and preach the Gospel to the ends of the Earth.

CHAPTER 10

Evangelists And Missions

As I looked out the window of a Boeing 767, I wondered if the Lord would open up any opportunities to share my faith when I got to China. I had heard of the underground, the state churches, and the voice from a friend that said, "they need evangelists in China." I recalled the official statement I had to sign saying I would not perform any duties pertaining to my occupation and wondered how the Lord would get around all that since I was an evangelist.

I had a lot of time to think about those things traveling five hundred sixty miles an hour, at thirty-five thousand feet, for over sixteen hours. Our family was traveling to pick up our soon-to-be adopted baby girl, Hannah. So many thoughts ran through my head, including fears, questions, and what exciting adventures lay ahead. I had never been to China before and wondered how I could relate to the Chinese people. I did not know the Chinese language, the culture or the people, much less any missionaries who were possibly there.

As I prayed about my own opportunities for ministry, I realized the need to communicate the needs and expectations of missionaries to evangelists and guest ministers, traveling abroad for ministry. We have heard about evangelists in general, but the area of missionary needs fulfilled by evangelists seems to have escaped much discussion.

The missionary evangelists active today are few and far between. The demands are great, and the sacrifices are many.

We often hear of pastors or stateside evangelists traveling abroad for ministry, and sadly the reason is often selfish and self-promoting. But what does the missionary need from an evangelist and how can the evangelist prepare for the rigors of cross-cultural ministry? Do we really need the evangelist, and if so what does an evangelist really do? How can a guest evangelist help facilitate a successful relationship with his or her host missionary or foreign pastor?

These are questions I will strive to answer with the goal of helping us see the role of the evangelist through the eyes of missions. I will include some experiences of what evangelists did that hurt missionaries the most, as well as things to think about and avoid while serving those who have pledged their lives to missionary service. I think one of the reasons this topic has so burdened my heart is that I see missionaries who only last for one term, due to the abuse of others.

THE NEED FOR EVANGELISTS

As evangelists work with local pastors for strengthening and helping congregations, so evangelists should be encouraged to work alongside missionaries fighting in the trenches of different cultures, wrestling new methods of communication within communities that may not accept a foreigner. There are many places that receive the "westerner" with open arms. In these situations, opportunities flourish for the missionary and evangelist; but even where acceptance is minimal, the evangelist can be a valuable resource of ministry to the missionaries of a particular country, community or individual. We can see a biblical example of this with the apostle Paul working with Timothy.

Evangelization involves the proclamation of the Gospel for the purpose of making converts, whether a one-on-one program like

"Evangelism Explosion,"[19] or in a mass presentation with crusades. No matter what the vehicle, the missionary needs evangelism skills and should feel the freedom and confidence in the resource of the evangelist. Incorporating the use of the evangelist allows the missionary to focus on the aspect of Christianization, or the discipling and spiritual formation of the believer who has come to faith in Jesus Christ. This discipling engages all areas of human growth: intellectual, emotional, as well as behavioral, and it demands extensive planning and prayer.

It is here that I believe evangelists have the vital opportunity to come alongside the missionary to not only preach good news to the sinner, make converts and baptize them; but also, to help revive the missionary, their family and their community of believers. We have seen the invaluable contribution evangelists have made in the American churches as congregations experience a fresh perspective and teaching from evangelists. Similarly, how much more could this same principle be implemented in the existing missionary works of the church.

THE EVANGELIST AND MISSIONARIES

One might think that "the nature of the evangelist's ministry can be seen in the meaning of the term itself – a bringer of good news."[20] But does the missionary see the evangelist as such? Assuredly there are great and not-so-great evangelists, but has the evangelist been a help to missionaries in general or has the name evangelist been tainted for good reason? We must remember that the evangelist is not, or should not be, competing against pastors or missionaries but is part of God's five-fold ministry to the Church. Churches, including ones in different countries, "need evangelists who are called, committed, compassionate, and concerned so that maximum benefit can be derived from their ministries."[21]

---

19 James Kennedy, "Evangelism Explosion: 'Reaching all the nations' and its impact on world missions," *Evangelical Missions Quarterly*, 33 (July 1997): 299.
20 Abbott, 7.
21 Ibid., 11.

I will build upon this presupposition with a note of caution. Cultures evolve and linguistics along with them, so today we can see quite a lot of overlap between the missionary, church planter, and evangelist. As a matter of fact, we see the apostle Paul functioning as "an apostle, prophet, evangelist, pastor, and teacher,"[22] with God using all five ministry gifts in Paul's itinerant work. And if an evangelist is one who "preaches the Gospel," then the apostles in Acts 8:4 and Jesus in Luke 20:1 were evangelists, according to the Greek verb *euaggelizo*; and in Ephesians 4:11, we see the word evangelist used to "denote an order of workers midway between apostles and prophets on the one hand, and pastors and teachers on the other."[23] We also see in Ephesians 4:12 that God's ministry gifts are "to prepare God's people for works of service so that the body of Christ may be built up."[24]

Ministry roles obviously have a tendency to overlap throughout the New Testament, which we can definitely see with the apostle Paul, but also again with Phillip. In Acts 21:8, we see Phillip, "the evangelist," but in Acts 6:5 he is also a deacon, called to be a minister of service in order to help the apostles. And in Acts 8 we see Phillip heading to Samaria to preach the Gospel, win converts and baptize the new believers, as we see with the Ethiopian eunuch in Acts 8:26.

In the New Testament scriptures, we see that the *kerygma*, or "the content of what was preached,"[25] becomes the main focus of Jesus' promise in Acts 1:8 as he emphasizes the Holy Spirit's role in the believer's continuing witness. It appears that the work and person of Jesus Christ are the emphases of the *kerygma*, as well as the eminence of Christ's return and baptism for all believers. Assuredly, the Lord uses the "foolishness of preaching" (I Cor 1:21) to bring about his salvation to the lost, whether through pastors, lay preachers, missionaries or evangelists.

---

22 Abbott, 11.

23 Donald Guthrie, "New Testament Theology," (Downers Grove: InterVarsity, 1981): 168.

24 *The New International Version*, (Grand Rapids: Zondervan), 1984.

25 Guthrie, 736.

They are all called to be evangelistic in some form or another in order that the lost may hear the Gospel, no matter what the cost. Missionary John York related how Melvin Hodges saw the "role of the missionary, in the beginning, to be that of an evangelist,"[26] since he or she brings the Gospel into a new place or culture, often paying a high price for the seeds sown. But then the missionaries move from the role of evangelists to that of teachers as they set out to teach and train more "Timothies" to do the work of an evangelist. Thus, we see the organism of the indigenous church at work: self-governing, self-supporting, and self-propagating.

This emphasis on the "indigenous" Church brought problems for some evangelists, especially within the Assemblies of God fellowship. As a matter of fact, in 1954, "the Foreign Missions Committee determined to grant publicity only to those evangelists who had worked in harmony with the missionaries overseas."[27] A problem arose over some missionary evangelists who would raise funds for the support of national pastors, and these evangelists would encounter "strong denunciation" from among the leaders within the Department of Missions. J. Philip Hogan, along with the Assemblies of God, believed that the indigenous church must stand by itself, even though sacrifice might be needed before it could "progress very far down the road toward being a stable, witnessing church."[28] This remains the ideology for the church today.

Billy Graham said in his fifteen affirmations which were made during the International Conference for Itinerant Evangelists in Amsterdam on July 1983 that evangelists should be willing to sacrifice and go wherever needed in order that "all peoples" might hear the Gospel. Affirmation two says: "We affirm our commitment to the Great Commission of our Lord, and we declare our willingness to

---

26 John V. York, "Missions in the Age of the Spirit," (Springfield: Logion, 1973): 155.

27 Gary B. McGee, "This Gospel Shall be Preached: A History and Theology of Assemblies of God Foreign Missions to 1959," (Springfield: Gospel Publishing House, 1986): 200.

28 Ibid., 201.

go anywhere, do anything, and sacrifice anything God requires of us in the fulfillment of that Commission."[29] At this same conference, a realization for the need of global evangelism reaffirmed itself when the evangelists present acknowledged the third affirmation, which said: "We respond to God's call to the biblical ministry of the evangelist, and accept our solemn responsibility to preach the Word to all peoples as God gives opportunity."[30]

In this third affirmation, we can see the support and realization by evangelists, that there is a need, opportunity and call to travel outside the borders of our own countries to boldly proclaim the Gospel of Jesus Christ to a world that is lost without Him.

These affirmations demand an understanding of ministry context and ability to communicate cross-culturally. Dr. James Kennedy planted a church with 17 people, and through his Evangelism Explosion program, grew to a congregation of over 8,000; with his material being used around the world "in more than 200 countries."[31] It is interesting to note, that after Evangelism Explosion had revamped itself, there was suddenly a "new emphasis on friendship and Discipling new believers."[32] Building friendships replicates the aspect of building bridges between cultures, and evangelists need to realize the importance of bridge building cross-culturally. Contextualization does not just "happen." One must devote themselves to a life of hard work within the confines of the Scriptures and culture.

The evangelist must also dedicate himself or herself to a life of prayer. There is an old saying that: "Business for God is not a substitute for time spent with God."[33] Without prayer, there will be no power, and

---

29 Billy Graham, 23.
30 Ibid., 31.
31 Kim A. Lawton, "Evangelism Explosion Retools Its Approach," *Christianity Today*, 41 (March 3, 1997): 58.
32 Ibid.
33 Abbott, 44.

you will become just another "business-person." True success remains in following the perfect will of God, especially in a cross-cultural setting where God's divine provision and protection are normative, everyday, basic needs. One of the greatest things an evangelist should remember is that ministries are built on relationships, and we need to treat missionaries and pastors the way we would want to be treated.

GUIDELINES FOR WORKING CROSS-CULTURALLY

There can be no doubt that a large part of an evangelist's ministry is to the pastor or missionary who invited them. The evangelist should always display an attitude of respect and appreciation for the opportunities afforded, and publicly, as well as privately, express honest appreciation for the one allowing them the opportunity to minister. The evangelist must remember that a missionary should not be told "how everything should be done or try to change their way of doing things."[34] Often the evangelist may not know the critical aspects of a particular people group and end up insulting the people as opposed to gaining respect, and converts. The missionary or overseas pastor remains the vital link for the people to whom God wants to speak, demonstrating his love and compassion for them.

The evangelist must remember that he or she speaks "for God, the church, and other evangelists. Even the Assemblies of God "Missions Manual" appropriately states that "everything the visiting minister says and does must be to further the cause for which missionaries have dedicated their entire lives."[35] They go on to say that their primary objective for "any" overseas ministry is "to complement the work of career missionaries,"[36] and if the Division of Foreign Missions feels

---

34 Abbott, 39.

35 "The Missions Manual," The Assemblies of God Division of Foreign Missions, (Springfield, Gospel Publishing House, 1995): 2-22.

36 Ibid., 2-16.

that an evangelist's ministry might be detrimental for any reason, that ministry will not be approved. Therefore, the goal of the evangelist must be to further the Kingdom of God, not any personal agenda, and remembering that they too are ambassadors for Jesus Christ and the rest of the "western" world.

A few years ago, I talked with Brother Cary Tidwell, a former Department head of foreign missions, who has since graduated to his heavenly home. Our conversation helped me gain a better insight into some vital safeguards to which the evangelist should adhere. Cary gave me three guidelines to help evangelists visiting a missionary or his or her family. The first was to be friendly and be a friend. Often missionaries may not have seen anyone for some time, and they may need to vent some steam from disappointments or situations encountered.

Do not take it personally, but realize that you are being far more than just a visitor—you are being a friend. The evangelist must also remember that missionaries travel extensively and often must move several times in their first stages of learning the culture and language. As a visiting evangelist, you must remember that missionaries have often left friends, family and loved ones for the rest of their lives if God so chooses. The evangelist may be the only "westerner" friend within a thousand miles and sensitivity to the missionary's feelings of "unsettlement" may be needed.

Similarly, Brother Tidwell said that probably the most precious aspect of a visiting minister or evangelist to the missionary is the "fellowship" that comes with any visit. It is during this time that evangelists may provide the greatest source of revitalization for the missionary and his or her family. Perhaps not with words of advice or wisdom, but in listening with a non-judgmental ear. As evangelists, we are often quick to speak and slow to listen, but the Lord admonishes us in James 1:19, "My dear brothers, take note of this: Everyone should be quick to listen, slow to speak and slow to become angry." Oftentimes the only requirement needed to bless others and bring comfort revolves around lips that are slow to speak and ears that are quick to hear.

Second, evangelists should be "open-minded." Refrain from arriving with a judgmental attitude, seeing everything from a "western" viewpoint. The evangelist who criticizes customs, leaders, techniques, churches or countries will most likely not be invited back.

The third guideline, confidentiality, is probably the most important. It cannot be stressed enough that struggles and disappointments shared with you must not be repeated. Men and women of God must be ministers of integrity. Otherwise we have become no better than the "reprobate" in Romans 1:29, known as "gossips" or "whisperers," which are an abomination to God.

The "western" evangelist must also guard against the mindset that motivations in other cultures will parallel motivations in their own country. Other religions may have more "materialistic" motivations for Christianity, as in the "power of western armies and navies in war surely makes the religion of these powerful foreigners better to have on your side than against you."[37]

Another problem arises in the hurdle of linguistics. The language of the people or culture you strive to minister in remains the artery of communicating the Gospel. When an evangelist arrives with an interpreter in hand, any problems that withstood the seasoned missionary will doubly withstand one unable to speak their language. Not only can linguistics distort the message, but "the meaning of the message can also be distorted by the image of the evangelist in the eyes of his audience."[38]

If for no other reason, the evangelist must adhere to the counsel of the missionary in all aspects of communication. If one is not careful, the message of the Gospel desired will not be the message delivered, much less received. In order to "contextualize" the message correctly,

---

37 Alan R. Tippett, "The Evangelization of Animists," *Perspectives: on the World Christian Movement*, 3rd ed. Eds. Winter, Ralph D. and Steven C. Hawthorne, (Pasadena: William Carey Library, 1981): 626.

38 Ibid., 628.

an evangelist must communicate with the missionary in residence to ascertain that proper theological truths are proclaimed in a socio-culturally acceptable manner.

There can be no doubt that miracles and wonders are very convincing avenues, which the Lord uses to convey His authenticity, especially in developing countries. But when signs and wonders begin manifesting themselves, every Godly leader is susceptible to pride. Therefore, "those used by God have the responsibility to deflect any honor and glory from themselves and onto the One who is the rightful recipient of praise—Jesus Christ."[39]

We can see the hazards of not giving God the glory in the biblical example of Herod, who was killed by an angel of the Lord and eaten by worms. Its imperative that the missionary, evangelist, or whoever is ministering "move quickly within the atmosphere of a miracle to relate spiritual truths that lead people to the knowledge of Christ."[40] If the missionary, or whoever is ministering, is not familiar with mighty moves of the Holy Spirit, this could be an avenue of devastating damage. We must expect the supernatural when ministering for God because Mark 16:20 tells us, "And they went forth, and preached every where, the Lord working with them, and confirming the word with signs following."

The evangelist must also be sensitive to the cultural issues, which may prevail in his or her given situation. This not only pertains to words spoken but even "your body language can also cause distress to the people,"[41] causing the Gospel message to fall upon deaf ears. This necessitates a humble spirit, which seeks guidance from the missionary, not a know-it-all mentality that disintegrates all the work that has taken years to develop. In many countries, just touching another person,

---

39 Steve Hill, "Confirming the Word with Signs & Wonders," *Enrichment*, 4 no. 1 (Winter 1999): 40.

40 Ibid.

41 Betty Jo Kenney, "The Missionary Family," (Pasadena: William Carey Library, 1983): 22.

even to shake hands or especially patting a child's head, is considered a serious offense, while in other cultures individuals walk arm in arm to show friendship. Many cultures also consider one hand to be "unclean," especially among those cultures that still eat with their fingers. The left hand may be designated for any "unclean" duties, while eating is done with the right hand. Thus, to offer a gift or handshake "with the unclean hand" is a tremendous insult.[42]

It is for this reason that when doubtful of your course of action, always inquire of your missionary or local pastor host. This should not be considered a weakness to avoid, but wisdom and a love for the people to whom you seek to minister, in order to help them see the Gospel message without being offensive. The greatest challenge for the evangelist or visiting clergy exists in presenting the Gospel in a contextualized manner so that those you minister to can relate it to their own personal lives.

Don't criticize the missionary from a material aspect while you are there. You do not realize all the difficulties involved with this missionary's situation and the sacrifices he or she may have already made to "become one" of the locals. You may encounter simple abodes with little furnishings, and visiting rodents wishing to keep you company at night. The church may have walls and a ceiling and it may not. You are not there to preach from a platform or a pulpit, but to a people who may have traveled many miles on foot just to hear this new teaching about the One they call Jesus.

Being critical is a terrible reflection upon you, as the visiting evangelist. I was once told a story of a pastor who went to preach in Cuba. The meat there is rationed, and only a few pounds are given to each person per year. At the first evening meal, they served beef and gave the pastor a huge serving. Only because the pastor had informed himself concerning some of the customs was he able to realize the sacrifice sitting before him. It was told that he almost could not eat the food before him,

---

42 Kenney, 24.

but ate while he wept, thanking them profusely. Every moment we can spend preparing ourselves for cross-cultural ministry will be a moment invested in a soul's eternal resting place. To think that our laziness could actually send someone to hell should be a wake-up call to all who travel abroad in ministry.

Something that you should not always expect in another culture is privacy. In many countries, "privacy is neither desirable nor understandable,"[43] with many servants or "helpers," living in the missionary's home. In China, there is no word for "privacy," and with over 1.2 billion people you might be able to understand why. Bathroom stalls are usually covered with a sheet, and "pit toilets" are the norm in Asian cultures, because "westerners" sit down to use the bathroom, while everyone else "squats." Additionally, your bed may only be a nice mat that lies on the floor. Although these may be "worse case" scenarios, it reveals the need for preparation and communication with your host.

You must also remember that you are a guest. Strive to be a blessing instead of a burden to those whom you have traveled thousands of miles to minister! Refrain from making demands upon the hosting family which are purely selfish in motive, like sightseeing, etc. If they offer to show you around that is one thing, but remember your call, your consideration, and your compassion—the missionary family needs that.

Another problem revolves around paying your own way. Often "hospitality rates" are expected rather than "posted" for your observance when staying with missionary families, and your perception of their situation may not always be accurate. For example, Betty Jo Kenney shares the following:

I know one missionary family who had to sell their air conditioner to pay the grocery bill for some evangelists who spent a month with them. Their mission clearly advises evangelists going overseas to "pay their own way," but these men said of their hosts, "They

---

43 Kenney, 75.

have plenty of money. They didn't ask us for any, and we ate like kings!" They never knew the family then had to manage in the constant heat without air conditioning for another year to pay for their guests' "royal meals."[44]

Here we see the stench that follows a pompous, self-seeking, ungrateful attitude! If you are served, you should offer to give something in return—at the very least a gift should be given.

Although the missionary life appears to be filled with exciting adventures, most likely that remains strictly an illusion. Jesus told us to follow his example and die "for the sheep" in John 10:11-15, and dying for the sheep often involves pain, sorrow, suffering and persecution. Even the apostle Paul suffered periods of being distraught outwardly, and at other times spiritually joyous as in 2 Corinthians 4:16. But sometimes "unbiblical" stress arises and brings havoc to the missionary's life; be it personal, relational within the family, or in the community at large. Stress can come from as serious a matter as losing a child to a misinterpretation of the light bill – but it is still stress.

One of the avenues of stress seems to lie in the "earthly ambition for success."[45] Although this reflects a "worldly" attitude, even in the church world there remains a well-fed fear of failure. Additionally, conflict can arise "on fields or between fields when missionaries compare lifestyle."[46] Missionaries, evangelists, pastors and every other clerical vocation falls under the shadow of the need to succeed. But, the true Christian is driven by a passion to see Jesus Christ exalted, refusing to let insecurities win the war when things appear to be less than perfect. Missionaries are just people, and evangelists have the opportunity to play a vital role in

---

44 Kenney, 91.
45 Ajith Fernando, "Some Thoughts on Missionary Burnout," *Evangelical Missions Quarterly*, 35, no. 4 (October 1999): 441.
46 John Sherwood, "The Missionary Lifestyle," *Evangelical Missions Quarterly*, 35 no. 3 (July 1999): 337.

the revitalization of missionaries, their families, and their communities when they find themselves in the valleys of life.

It remains a fact, that when one suffers along with another, respect is gained. But, when the missionary or evangelist fail to suffer alongside of the people to whom they seek to minister, the very people their heart is burdened for often take advantage of them. If comfort and prosperity remain our primary objectives, missionaries and missionary evangelists alike will be despised. And while it never seems pleasant to suffer, the evangelist has a chance to make a difference in a missionary's life by suffering alongside them.

This difference can lead to fruitful years ahead if we are sensitive to God's leading, or another dead branch, if we selfishly seek to glorify ourselves and our ministries. Probably one of our greatest challenges manifests itself in the aspect of "suffering joyfully," even as the apostle Paul shares with us in Colossians 1:24.

SUMMARY

At the World Council of Churches in 1989, there was a proclamation that all other "non-Christian religions are as good as (if not better than) the best of Christianity."[47] If this is really the case, then the only conceivable objectives become "dialogue and cross-fertilization," and we would truly become the pluralistic society that so many desire. But it is the Christian missionary who remains our frontline defense abroad against the pollution of the Gospel and pluralism, and not only the missionary but also the entire "five-fold" ministries. God has given the Church what it needs to succeed, and it remains our responsibility to fulfill our obligation, working arm-in-arm to fulfill the great commission. If we do our part, God will undoubtedly do His.

---

47 Tokunboh Adeyemo, "Whatever Happened to Evangelism?" *Christianity Today*, 37 (April 5, 1993): 34.

If evangelists are to come alongside and undergird the efforts of the missionary, they must maintain a servant attitude. Too often evangelists head to the field, expecting everyone else to bow graciously and roll out the red carpet, without the slightest thought of the financial burden this places on the missionary or the ramifications of a "westerner" mindset. The missionary has been called of God and supported by saints of God "believing" in them to spend their money with frugality, striving to "contextualize" the Gospel of Jesus Christ to a world that is lost. The office of the evangelist was created to "serve" the Church, and that is exactly what we must strive to do, whether the church is in North America, or in the "uttermost parts of the earth."

In centuries past, we can see numerous times when great moves of the Spirit upon whole nations started with an obedient evangelist, and as we partner with the missionary of today may our prayer echo the apostle Paul's in 1 Corinthians 9:22b, "I have become all things to all men so that by all possible means I might save some." Truly, it is not about personal agenda or acclaim, but about proclaiming and exalting that name which is above every name – Jesus Christ.

CHAPTER 11

Can I Really Make It?

ome candid conversation needs to take place regarding whether a full-time evangelistic ministry can survive today financially. Many ministry leaders desire to encourage individuals who feel the call of ministry and will exhort you to pursue that call with all your strength. Perhaps some ulterior motives drive this encouragement, but most ministry leaders have a sincere desire to help you succeed. After all, it is the call of God that you strive to hear and heed, so you must ultimately seek God for His leading and direction.

REALITY #1 = YOU MUST KNOW THAT YOU ARE CALLED

I recently sat down with a budding evangelist who still had another year of Bible college to finish before heading out into full-time ministry. He was so excited about what God was doing in his ministry and how God was providing for his ministry needs. He even shared some specifics about a mission trip to South America that he had recently completed. God miraculously used a person within his circle of friends and relationships to come through for the final portion of expenses related to this particular mission trip. I shared my delight with him at God's provision, but then I asked him: "That just covered the trip expenses, though, right?" He answered in the affirmative. I then added some additional thoughts:

"So, you probably still live at home, right?"

"Yes."

"And there wasn't any additional provision for paying bills and taking care of obligations here, right?"

"Yeah."

"So, since you are getting married you will also need to think about taking care of your spouse, right?

"Uh-huh."

"So, all you did was pay for the cost of the trip. There was no money left over to help with living once you got back, right?"

"Right."

Admittedly, I am pretty hard on new folks who ask me about how to become an evangelist. I try to share the blunt truth of how hard it is to stay on the field of ministry without additional revenue streams of support. If I fail to scare my new inquirers, then I conclude that they must be truly called of God. If I can scare them out of evangelistic ministry, then I conclude their initial zeal evolved from an emotional altar call appeal, or some other person of influence trying to steer their lives according to their own wishes instead of God's.

I cannot reiterate enough, the importance and enormity of this decision of calling. You must take a real look at your life and assets to determine whether this is indeed a calling or just a desire. A desire is admirable, but it is not a calling. "How do I know if it is a calling or desire?"

That is a great question! You will know that it is a calling because of two major things: First, you find that you cannot do anything else. All you think about, dream about, and act on evolves around the call of sharing the Gospel with others.

Second, there will be fruit to confirm your ministry calling. That means that you will often be surprised by the number of people who respond to altar calls for a salvation decision—without manipulation—or by the manifestation of the spiritual gifts if you sense the call to a revivalist type of ministry.

To illustrate, I have a friend who has the unquestionable calling of an evangelist. Everywhere this brother goes he is talking to people about Christ and leading them to salvation decisions. This is not his own doing, but clear evidence that the Holy Spirit works through him to bring others to a knowledge of Jesus Christ. When I hang out with him, waitresses make decisions for Christ; salvation invitations are given on public transportation, in parks, stores, and any other place where this brother senses a platform exists to share the Gospel message. Hanging around this brother is exciting—yet sometimes intimidating!

This fruitfulness also finds evidence in those who sense God's call to be a revivalist. This aspect of evangelistic ministry mirrors the Old Testament prophets who called the Church back to a right relationship with God. Oftentimes, healing, prophecy, and other ministry gifts manifest themselves within the context of a revivalist or prophetic ministry. These men and women have a burden for the wounded Church and seek to encourage and minister to those within the Church in order to strengthen that body of believers for "works of service" (NIV) or "the work of the ministry" (KJV) within their community (Eph. 4:12). But, no matter whether you sense the call to evangelistic or revivalist ministry, God will confirm the call by fruitfulness in your ministry.

So, now that you know you have been called of God, how do you make this vocation pay for itself? If that is your first question, you need to head to the prayer closet and ask God for a heart change! In ministry, it seems as though money flows out almost faster than it flows into the bank. That is why a heart change is necessary—it is God's ministry, and He is the one who helps us take care of the financial responsibility.

Truthfully, we write the checks and pay the bills, but God alone provides the open doors of opportunity and financial blessings to keep His ministries afloat. When you know that you are called, you will have the faith to believe that God is indeed your source of all financial sustenance and that he will come through again and again. George Mueller discovered this timeless truth with all the ministry opportunities God provided for him, and we must embrace this same mentality—God is enough. That said, there are some additional realities that I want to share with you in the paragraphs ahead.

REALITY #2 = TRAVEL EXPENSES ARE HUGE

If itinerant ministers could find a way to pay for the expense of travel they could probably live on their offerings. The expense of travel today—from planes to automobiles—continues to climb. Even when you drive your own vehicle, there are hidden expenses. The Internal Revenue Service even understands that fact and gives those in business and charitable work a mileage expense deduction when driving your own vehicle. A ministry cliché that finds truth far too often is that "they will fly you before they will drive you." This cliché vocalizes the reality that a church will often pay for the price of airfare before they even think about reimbursing you for miles driven to arrive at their location.

The problem is that most itinerant ministers starting out in ministry will not be flying. When you are new to the ministry not many people know you, so why would they spend a lot of money to have someone they do not know come and minister to their congregation? The reality is that they won't, so driving to locations where ministry opportunities exist remains your primary mode of transportation initially.

One way to address the need for mileage reimbursement is through your contact letter that is sent approximately one month prior to your service (see chapter five). In this letter, you can graciously say at some point: "Would you please pray with us that God would help us with our mileage/travel expenses?" You don't have to elaborate, but you can include this in other items of prayer that are crucial to the success of your time with that particular church. You do not want to appear only concerned with finances, but mainly for God's blessing upon the service.

Additional financial burdens will distract from God's best, but don't make demands or appear pushy—that's a good way not to be invited back! If the church leader is open to helping you, this will encourage future dialog about the subject, but if they are not open to this then just leave it alone. Here is where you retreat to your prayer closet and allow God time to keep your heart pure. God knows how to take care of His servants and it remains our responsibility to stay true to Him.

Incorporating your ministry can be another way to help with travel expenses. This is not a quick, thoughtless endeavor, but one that must be made through prayer and the counsel of others. If you sense that itinerant ministry will be your long-term ministry venue, then incorporating may be the path for you. This gives the ministry added validity to some and provides an opportunity to keep the ministry accounting totally separate from your personal affairs. Incorporating, followed by gaining a 501(c)3 non-profit status, will allow you to enlist supporters who believe in your ministry and desire to help you financially.

God has blessed many with the ability to make money, while others he has blessed with the opportunity and gifting to go and preach the Gospel. Everyone contributing to your ministry shares in the burden and blessing of all that you do through your ministry. Each state in the United States has somewhat different guidelines for incorporating and gaining a non-profit status, so be sure to check with your state's Secretary of State web page for the latest requirements and fees.

A third way to help with travel expenses comes from product sales. Leaving your ministry behind in DVDs, CDs, books and other products remains a wonderful way to sow the Gospel seed. However, care must be made to avoid overemphasizing the product table at the expense of your time and opportunity of ministry to the people. If needed, some itinerant ministers ask the church for a table and person to assist them. They provide the church with resources, as well as a moneybag or box with about $40 in small bills to make change for the person managing the table.

Itinerant ministers, who have ministry products, often have family back home or publishers, send a certain amount of product to the churches wherein they will minister that week. The hazard, I say again unapologetically, lies in being seen as a "hireling" who cares more about money than ministry. Sometimes it's best to share the cost of a product or give a suggested donation to the ministry for certain things on your product table.

An additional challenge for new evangelists lies in not having any product to sell until your ministry has functioned for a few years. Audio and video recordings of your ministry usually come from larger churches that have quality equipment. If music ministry is your strength, you will need to find an affordable recording studio that can provide quality products. Itinerant ministers involved in drama, children's evangelism and a few other specialized ministries have the added challenge of purchasing or making new props for their ministry every year or two.

A fourth and rather common way to take care of travel expenses is for you or your spouse to work a secular or part-time job—especially when you are getting started. There are viable jobs that can be staffed while traveling, but care must be taken to keep from neglecting the ministry. Sometimes seasonal jobs avail themselves to an itinerant minister around holiday seasons when additional temporary employees are needed by area businesses. Bi-vocational ministers are in abundance across the entire globe and include not only itinerant ministers but church leaders as well. That is why I always tell new evangelists not to quit their jobs until they become so busy in ministry that there is no other option.

Whatever option you sense God leading you to embrace, do it with excellence and without whining. If you are prone to whining about circumstance and misfortune, then please do not enter the ministry. The ministry involves facing the greatest spiritual battles you can imagine, so if you are looking for an easy line of work, please look elsewhere. You are a minister—one who will be used, abused, talked about, pressured, extorted, defrauded, and seemingly underfunded. But our reward is not of this Earth—there is a Heavenly Kingdom that we will call home and that is where our treasure will await those of us who call ourselves Christian. I pray that you will be among us.

REALITY #3 = DEBT WILL DESTROY YOU

Several years ago, I had a young man call me and declare their belief that God had called them to evangelistic ministry. After further conversation, I discovered that he was having difficulties in his current ministry position and did not get along with the pastor...hum. After even further conversion he revealed that he had gone to Bible College and also attended seminary on student loans in order to gain his master's degree. As prestigious as that all may sound, this young man owed approximately $100,000 in student loans alone!

I told the young man that there was no way that he could service that kind of debt load on an evangelist budget. The payment on a loan of that size would take every penny that a new evangelist could even hope to earn in a year's time. He would realistically need to find some secular employment if he honestly wanted to pay down that debt. Even many current ministry positions would not afford this young man the resources necessary to survive and repay his student loans.

I understand the need for many to acquire loans in order to finish undergraduate education. However, to go ahead and pursue a master's degree prior to paying off your existing debt seems a bit irresponsible. As Christians, we have a divine obligation to pay back loans that we legally obtain with a commitment to repay. Walking away from a loan should never be an option for a Christian. I understand there may be extenuating circumstances that are an exception to this rule of conduct, but it should definitely not be the normal attitude we embrace.

So, what do you do when you have a financial need and resources are not available to you? You go to your prayer closet. Early in our ministry, we purchased a newer used truck to pull our fifth-wheel and accommodate an additional child. About six months into our ownership the radio and CD player started acting up. We had a portable CD and tape player that started having a permanent seat in the front of our truck.

I decided that we needed to get the radio fixed and took it to a radio repair shop for an estimate, where I received the sobering news that it would cost approximately $110 for repairs. I got back in my truck and started driving home. I was so depressed that I started talking to God with a conversation something like this: "God, I don't have $10 much less $110. I don't know what to do! You told us to buy this truck, and now we can't even practice our music since the radio and CD player are broken. That's just not right God. (Ever have conversations with the Creator of the universe like that?)

I stopped by a filling station so that I could buy myself a soda…yep, I didn't have the $10, but I was willing to spend $1 on a soda to wallow in my discouragement! This was the time when soda bottles had a cap that might have prizes underneath. I was so depressed that I thought, "Well, maybe I'll get a free soda"—Definitely not the man full of faith and power. When I twisted the cap off and looked underneath, it said: "You have just won $100." What? I was so full of appreciation for God's provision (not really) that I had to ask the clerk behind the counter: "Does that really mean I won $100?"

"Yes, sir. Congratulations man."

I couldn't believe my ears! I got back in my truck and let out a good old fashion Texas yell and started shouting my praises to the God who so graciously provided—in spite of my complaining only a few moments earlier. God came through—and God continues to come through for his children as we abandon our own abilities and seek him with our whole heart. He will show us what to do and help in time of need.

REALITY #4 = CUT COSTS
EVERYWHERE YOU CAN

It constantly amazes me how money seems to have wings and flies away! Whenever I receive some additional funds there always seems to be a need that arises at the same time. God graciously helps us in our ministries, but we do need to be good stewards of what we receive and instill some disciplines that will help us keep our expenses to a minimum. Here are a few things that Nancy and I do to help cut our expenses while traveling.

Pack a lunch. Whenever we start out via our vehicle, Nancy always packs sandwiches and snacks to help keep from spending money at fast food restaurants. This also helps us eat healthily and keeps us from overindulging at restaurants. I also try to buy groceries to satisfy any hunger temptations during revival meetings if I plan on fasting a bit during the week. I talk with the pastor on what they normally do and try to fit into their schedule. I normally eat a larger meal at lunch and skip the evening meal so that I do not have to preach on a full stomach.

Then I may just grab a snack with the pastor after the service or head back to my hotel or evangelist's quarter for a snack from some of my groceries. Try to keep from being a burden on the pastor and that congregation—often called being "low maintenance." We also try to avoid arriving right on time for the evening meal so that the pastor does not feel pressured to take us out to eat.

The pastor may truly want to get together, and that is fine, but you must strive to keep from falling into the practice of expecting or manipulating others to take you out to eat the evening before your services start. If your services start in the evening, this may not be applicable, but just be sensitive to the fact that you should be a "low maintenance" blessing.

Look for deals. When booking flights, try to shop online for great deals several months in advance. There are numerous websites that cater to the frequent flier. You should also look for flights from airports around you if you do not live in a major metropolitan area with an international airport. Sometimes smaller airports can fly you cheaper with an additional flight than you can get driving to a major city and flying out of the international airport! Rental cars operate the same way, and shopping around can be very rewarding. Loyalty programs can be very advantageous if there is a particular airline that operates near you.

Clothing is another area where deals can be plentiful. My wife, Nancy, has found $100 dresses for $2 at used clothing stores. Thankfully, Nancy and the rest of my children love the "hunt" for new clothes at bargain prices. They usually don't even like to go to the malls or even outlet malls unless they have an after-Christmas sale with 75% off! They have helped me find discount suit shops and bargain brand name shoes for a fraction of what they would normally cost. I do believe you should dress professionally and try your best to dress with excellence, but there are wonderful bargains to be found online and in the local communities where you may minister. The pastor and/or his wife may even love the thrill of thrift store shopping and be elated that he or she can take someone along!

Make you own. As I shared earlier in the book, when we first started in ministry, we created our own ministry poster with colored poster stock from a local store. Then we would glue our ministry card on the poster. Not the cutting-edge materials that are available today, but many of the small churches where we started appreciated them. Now, you can email bulletin inserts, PowerPoint displays, and other items for church leaders to share with their people about you. Some stores even sell video cards where you can record a personal message if you have that kind of money to spend. Whatever you do be creative and don't feel like you need to have the latest posters, gadgetry, and media presentations when you first start out.

Take advantage of FREE. Today, there are many free resources that you can take advantage of to help you in your ministry. Free websites and email services abound, along with extremely cheap ministry prayer cards and even free ministry tracts. The Assemblies of God fellowship provides free websites for their evangelists and inclusion in an online directory where pastors can search by name, ministry emphasis, city, state, credentialing district or even ministry dates. Other organizations have listings of their evangelists and sometimes, local districts do as well. Work to find the free resources that might be a blessing to you by elevating the visibility of your ministry.

REALITY #5 = EXPECT GOD TO DO THE MIRACULOUS

I share all of these situations, ideas, and options for ministry because you need to think through the challenges and make a plan. If you are married, you need to involve your spouse and mutually agree on how to proceed in ministry. If either you or your spouse cannot agree on how the ministry will function, then you cannot expect to thrive in ministry, because God is not the author of confusion or division in your marriage. I am not sure who originally quoted this, but it has been said: "If you fail to plan, you plan to fail."

Planning with your spouse is paramount, and if you are single, you must think through how you will avoid difficult situations that you might encounter. Another great saying is: "We need to work as though everything depended on us and pray as though everything depended on God." When we enter ministry with this humble attitude, we will find favor in the most unlikely places.

IN SUMMARY

The Spirit empowered evangelist is one who totally surrenders to the Holy Spirit's leading. Acts 1:8 reveals that the Holy Spirit has been given to empower us for service—a divine service that can only be fully accomplished by allowing the Holy Spirit prominence in our lives. When the Holy Spirit leads and guides your life, ministry, schedule, finances, family, or any other area of your life, you find God's grace and help when things get uncomfortable.

You will undoubtedly face plenty of unpleasant folks over the years—these people need the Gospel most of all. God has entrusted you with the most precious gift he has to give his children—the glorious message of how to restore a right relationship with Him. He loves His children and continues to search for those who will answer the unique call of evangelist. May you rise and say like Isaiah did in chapter six verse eight: "Here am I; send me."

However, I remember a friend saying once that it's "all about the call." Those words continually echo in my ears as I endeavor to put on the whole armor of God (Ephesians 6:10) every day so that I can "fight the good fight of faith" (1 Timothy 6:12) in the spiritual battles that assail me at times. I must admit that over the years, I have wanted to quit—just lay down the spiritual sword and walk away.

But, it's about the call of God. He won't let you quit—and if you listen closely—you will hear the Holy Spirit's encouraging whisper, much like a gentle breeze that will bring healing and restoration, or like early morning dewdrops upon a yearning blade of grass. You may feel so insignificant, but in God's eyes, you are one of His cherished children. You will face daunting circumstances and wade through discouragement in this vocation of ministry. But when you wait upon the Holy Spirit and follow his leading you will hear those cherished words: "Well done, thou good and faithful servant" (Matthew 25:21).

I hope you will embrace the gift of the evangelist if you sense God calling you to be a purveyor of the good news—the Gospel. And I pray that you found this book helpful in some small way. May God bless you richly as you seek to be the Spirit-empowered evangelist he has called you to be—no matter where he calls you to go.

APPENDIX A

RESUME

Your Name

PO Box or Street Address
City / State / Zip
Phone# (Home)
Phone# (cell)

Rev. Pastor's Name
c/o Church name
PO Box or Street Address
City / State / Zip

Pastor _____,

Here is some additional information, and references, for your convenience and confirmation (**Limit to two pages maximum**).

Personal Data

Family Names and ages

Professional Preparation

Graduate:	Name of School
Military Service:	If any
Ministry Training:	List from most recent to oldest – only use 2-4

Christian Service

Conversion: Rededicated 1987
                          Baptism in the Holy Spirit 1988
                          Called to the ministry 1990
Presently: Evangelistic Ministry - music and preaching
Present Occupation: Full-time evangelist – Assemblies of God credentials
                          – Ordained 2005

References (list name = 4-8 should be plenty, and contact info only – save endorsements or write-ups for your website or if asked. Pastors are busy, and you don't need to give them a pile of paperwork to read through)

Thank you again for your time, and if you have any questions, please feel free to email or call.

For Him,
SIGNATURE
Your printed name
Today's date

APPENDIX B

POSTER LETTER

Your Design Here

Today's date

Rev. Pastor's Name
c/o Church name
PO Box or Street Address
City / State / Zip

Pastor _____,

Greetings in the name of the Lord!

I am sending some ministry posters for you and praying that things are going well for you there in _____. Things are busy as ever here with ministry, family, and just getting settled back into some sort of routine after our summer travels, but as usual God is always there to help get us through!

I want to thank you again for allowing us the opportunity to minister for the Lord in song and the Word on **Ministry Date** in the morning and evening services. Nancy, Joshua, Hannah and I look forward to being with you all there, and we are praying God's perfect plan come to pass for these services.

I will try to give you a call a week or two prior to our scheduled date to check in with you, but if you have any questions or need further information, please don't hesitate to email or call. My cell phone is probably the best way to reach me. You can also visit our website at www.yourown which God has graciously given to us, in order to stay abreast of all that the Lord is doing in our lives.

May God continue to bless you richly!

Your brother in Christ,

John "Bubba" Doe

"A favorite Scripture verse here or mission statement"

Phone: (123) 456-7890 | Email: bubba1@someisp
Website: www.yourown | AGWM Acct# 123456

APPENDIX C

HOUSING ALLOWANCE DESIGNATION

Rev. Your Name
PO Box or Street where you live
Your City / State / Zip

To Whom It May Concern:

Thank you for allowing me the privilege of preaching the Gospel of Jesus Christ to your wonderful congregation.

Please designate my honorarium for ministering to your congregation as follows:

Housing Allowance (50% of the total below)   _____

Mileage Reimbursement (Jan 1, 2016 IRS rate is ****¢) __N/A__

Taxable Compensation   _____

Total Honorarium   _____

Thank you for helping us ensure proper accounting procedures are followed as we serve the share the wonderful Gospel of Jesus Christ

May God's richest blessings be yours,
Your Name

Acknowledged and authorized by: (church pastor / personnel where you minister)

_____   _____

(Print Name)   (Title)

_____   _____

(Signature)   (Date)

APPENDIX D

CONFIRMATION LETTER

Your Design Here

Today's date

Rev. Pastor's Name

c/o Church name
PO Box or Street Address
City / State / Zip

Pastor _____,

Greetings in the name of the Lord!

I pray things are going well for you and that your schedule isn't too hectic there in _____. Things are pretty hectic here, with my "honey-do" list and everything else going on, but as usual, God has been extremely faithful!

I wanted to confirm and thank you for allowing us the opportunity to minister for the Lord on **Ministry Date** in the morning service and for the hotel accommodations. Nancy, Joshua, Hannah and I look forward to seeing everyone there, and we are praying God's perfect plan come to pass for this service. I am also looking forward to sharing a little bit about our mission trips to Africa.

I will try to give you a call a week or two prior to our scheduled date to check in with you, but if you have any questions or need further information, please don't hesitate to email, text, or call – my cell phone is still the best way to catch me. You can also visit our website at www.

yourown which God has graciously given to us, in order to stay abreast of all that the Lord is doing in our lives and ministry.

May God continue to bless you richly!

Your brother in Christ,

John "Bubba" Doe

"A favorite Scripture verse here or mission statement"

Phone: (123) 456-7890 | Email: bubba1@someisp
Website: www.yourown | AGWM Acct# 123456

APPENDIX E

INTRO / CONFIRMATION LETTER

Your Design Here

Today's date

Rev. Pastor's Name
c/o Church name
PO Box or Street Address
City / State / Zip

Pastor _____,

I wanted to let you know that I enjoyed visiting with you on the phone this past week, and I so appreciate you allowing us the opportunity to minister for the Lord on **Ministry Date** in revival services – even if Brother Smith did tell me to call☺. I am sending you some information about myself with references and a current schedule, as well as a ministry card for your convenience.

As far as our ministry, (spouse's name if applicable) and I define our ministry as a ministry of encouragement, restoration, and healing for the entire body of Christ. To let those saints that are hurting know that God has not forsaken them and that He still cares about even their smallest need. "Meeting people where they are" and "looking to see those that others don't see" are some of our mottoes as we strive to tell others about having a relationship with a Savior who cares, through singing and preaching God's Word. We passionately seek to help heal the hurting, and we believe the Lord is using us to be a ministry of encouragement, education, and empowerment through the principles of His Word.

Realizing that pastors are extremely busy, I want to thank you for your time, and I pray the Lord will continue to bless you and your church family in this new millennium. I look forward to seeing you in the near future, and if you have any questions or need further information, please don't hesitate to email or call. My cell number is probably the best way to reach me.

May God continue to bless you richly!

Your brother in Christ,

John "Bubba" Doe

"A favorite Scripture verse here or mission statement"

Phone: (123) 456-7890 | Email: bubba1@someisp
Website: www.yourown | AGWM Acct# 123456

APPENDIX F

5ᵀᴴ WHEEL CHECKLIST

Here are just a few items of importance that you should make sure you do when hooking up any fifth wheel travel trailer. Many of these items are applicable to pull-type travel trailers as well. These are just a few thoughts of my own, and you should make a checklist for yourself. Over time we get a bit over-confident! I've seen more than one tailgate that someone forgot to lower before backing up to their fifth-wheel trailer—and a trailer that was damaged because someone forgot to raise the tailgate after the trailer was hooked up!

- Prepare inside – electric off
- Frig off
- Chalk wheels
- Lower tailgate
- Unlatch hitch
- Back up to hitch on 5th wheel
- Raise/lower hitch
- Connect to 5th wheel
- Release latch – make sure safety latch on lower 5th wheel is raised/ stands up
- Store chalk blocks (if used) in truck
- Hook up electric
- Hook up brake safety cable
- Shut tailgate
- Check lights
- Side mirrors on truck extended
- Load 5th wheel (water, clothes, etc…)

If you sense that the Holy Spirit has spoken into your life and ministry through this book and you believe it would be a helpful addition to someone's library, please help us distribute it to as many people as possible. Write today for ordering information and quantity discounts.

Marshall M. Windsor
PO Box 9907
Tyler, TX 75711

mail@marshallwindsor.com

Connect Online
www.marshallwindsor.com
www.windsmin.org

ABOUT THE AUTHOR

Marshall Moore Windsor was born in Dallas, Texas, but spent much of his early years on the family farm in Missouri. A love of the outdoors and no stranger to hard work, Marshall pitched in with his seven siblings to help keep the family farm running. Fishing and frog hunting were some of his favorites pastimes when he wasn't cleaning horse stalls, hauling hay, working cattle, or helping get crops in or out of the fields.

Marshall graduated from Texas A&M University with a BS in Mechanized Agriculture prior to entering the United States Army as a Field Artillery officer in 1983. It was during Marshall's time in military service that he rededicated his life to God.

Marshall and Nancy sold their farm in 1999 and moved to Springfield, Missouri to attend the one-year Bible program at Central Bible College, and step out into evangelistic ministry. Marshall received both his Master of Divinity degree in the area of biblical languages and his Doctor of Ministry degree in the area of evangelism and discipleship from The Assemblies of God Theological Seminary. Marshall served as an adjunct professor of evangelism from 2007 to 2011 at Central Bible College and from 2008 to 2011 at the Assemblies of God Theological Seminary in Springfield, Missouri. Marshall and Nancy transitioned to East Texas where they reside with their family and base their ministry today.

In 2005 Marshall was appointed as the National Evangelist Representative for the Assemblies of God fellowship and has counted it an extreme privilege to serve as the Evangelist General Presbyter, representing all those men and women who have sacrificed to follow the call of God into evangelistic ministry. Marshall and his family minister around the world, and continue to teach and train young evangelists, in order to fulfill God's Great Commission.

Note from the Publisher

Are you a first time author?

Not sure how to proceed to get your book published?
Want to keep all your rights and all your royalties?
Want it to look as good as a Top 10 publisher?
Need help with editing, layout, cover design?
Want it out there selling in 90 days or less?

Visit our website for some exciting new options!

www.chalfant-eckert-publishing.com